CELEBRATE SPECIAL DAYS

by

Phyllis Hand

illustrated by Judy Hierstein and Kathryn Hyndman

Cover by Dan Grossmann

Shining Star Publications, Copyright © 1985
A Division of Good Apple, Inc.

ISBN No. 0-86653-280-3

Standardized Subject Code TA ac

Printing No. 98765432

Shining Star Publications
A Division of Good Apple, Inc.
Box 299
Carthage, IL 62321-0299

Unless otherwise indicated, the King James version of the Bible was used in preparing the activities in this book.

DEDICATION

To Ken and Rachel Vandenhoek . . . in appreciation
of their dedication to children.

TO THE TEACHER

"This is the day which the Lord hath made; we will rejoice and be glad in it."   Psalm 118:24

God meant for every day to be special. As teachers, we have the opportunity to use in unique ways the abilities and materials God has given to us to make every day meaningful for the children. By making learning exciting, we will instill in young students the thrill of studying God's Word that will last a lifetime. The activities suggested in this book will help to make every day God has given us a very special day.

Variety is the key to good teaching. Many different kinds of activities are included to meet the learning styles of children. The plays need no specific props. However, if some costumes are used, the play becomes more meaningful and is more fun to perform. The other children in the class may be involved as the audience. Younger children could also be used as an audience for your performance. The games can be used to reinforce learning. These should be as bright and attractive as possible. They could be placed on a convenient table so that the children may play them when they arrive in the morning. The games may also be used as group activities. The bulletin boards are designed so the children make a contribution to them. To make creative writing and artistic endeavor memorable experiences, make a booklet for each child, and paste each story, poem, or drawing on a separate page. When the books are full, the children may take them home as keepsakes. Because individual papers handed back to children often do not arrive home, parents miss out on one of the treasures of their young one's childhood experiences. The booklets help to solve this problem.

Recognition of good work encourages one to do even better. Awards should be used extensively to make the children aware of their accomplishments in tangible ways.

JANUARY

1 Become a new person. II Cor. 5:17	**2** Read a chapter in the New Testament.	**3** Learn about the new heaven. Isaiah 65:17

4 Sing a new song.	**5** Find out about Abraham's new land.	**6** Make a new friend.	**7** Take a new person to Sunday School.	**8** Be responsible for a new job at home.

9 Play a new game.	**10** Ask someone to tell you about Joseph's new coat.	**11** Let your friend be first today.	**12** Find out about the first family.	**13** Ask your teacher about Solomon's new temple.	**14** Draw a new picture for your Sunday School teacher.	**15** Read about the first rainbow. Genesis 9:8-17
16 Share a treat with a new friend.	**17** Find out about the first Jewish person.	**18** Draw a new invention.	**19** Be the first one up today.	**20** Say a new prayer for lunch.	**21** Pray for your new friend.	**22** Be first to obey your teacher.
23 Read about the first miracle of Jesus. John 2	**24** Have someone read to you about the first prayer. Genesis 4:26	**25** Be the first one ready for school.	**26** Find out about the first child.	**27** Think about your new blessings.		
28 Learn a new Bible verse.	**29** Be first to smile at someone today.	**30** Thank God for the new day.				
31 Read about the first skyscraper. Genesis 11						

Shining Star Publications, Copyright © 1985, A division of Good Apple, Inc.

CELEBRATE THE NEW YEAR

"... I will bless thee ... and thou shalt be a blessing."

Genesis 12:2

TURN OVER A NEW LEAF

January is the month when people like to make new beginnings in their lives. It can be exciting to see a brand new year ahead of us. Resolutions are often made to try to break old habits or to improve one's self in a particular way. Resolutions are usually directed inwardly. However, God intended for us to have an outward look. He has blessed us so that we can be a blessing to others. Change the focus of resolutions by teaching the children to recognize the blessings God has given to them—health, strength, love, talents, freedoms, or good dispositions. Have them list their blessings. Encourage them to find ways to use the blessings God has given them to be blessings to other people.

MOLDING YOUNG LIVES

"... children are an heritage of the Lord: and the fruit of the womb is his reward."

Psalm 127:3

Each child is a gift from God. Help children to recognize their unique places in the world. Challenge them to use the gift of life God has given them to make this year one of the best because they followed God's plan. Help them to find ways to be reflections of God's love. One way would be to start a new chart everyday. At the top, write: Yesterday I showed God's love by .... Below this statement have the children list their ways of showing love. Discuss the chart at the end of each day.

BLESSED TO BE A BLESSING

These are my blessings:

_____
_____
_____

This year I will be a blessing by:

_____
_____
_____

Yesterday I showed God's love by:

_____
_____
_____
_____
_____

HAPPY NEW YEAR

"This is the day which the Lord hath made; we will rejoice and be glad in it."   Psalm 118:24

CARE OF NEW BABIES

". . . this shall be a sign unto you; Ye shall find the babe wrapped in swaddling clothes, lying in a manger."   Luke 2:12

In the days of Jesus, babies were not allowed to kick and stretch. Instead, the babies were wrapped tightly in swaddling bands. The arms were pressed closely to the body. The legs were tucked tightly together. The mother then took long, thin strips of cloth and wrapped them around the baby. To find out how a baby might look, have the children wrap a doll in long, thin strips of fabric. When finished, the doll should look similar to the picture.

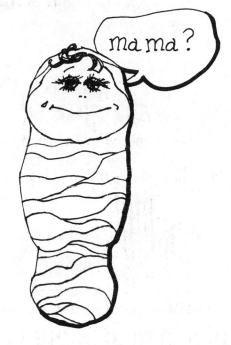

NEW BLESSINGS EVERY DAY

"It is of the Lord's mercies that we are not consumed, because his compassions fail not. They are new every morning: great is thy faithfulness."   Lamentations 3:22, 23

The Bible tells us that God provides new blessings every day. Help the children to recognize the blessings God gives them each day. Encourage them to share the blessings with their friends and their families.

DEDICATE YOUR HOUSE TO GOD

". . . What man is there that hath built a new house, and hath not dedicated it?"   Deuteronomy 20:5a

It was the custom in Bible times to dedicate a new house to God. Help each child plan a dedication party to have at his house. Before the guests leave, the child should pray a special prayer for the house, blessing the people who live in the house and thanking God for all of the wonderful times people will enjoy in the house.

GOD BLESS OUR HOME

IS THERE ANYTHING NEW UNDER THE SUN?

"Is there any thing whereof it may be said, See, this is new? it hath been already of old time, which was before us." Ecclesiastes 1:10

MAKE A NEW PAIR OF SHOES

Sandals were worn by most of the people in Bible times. Sandals had either wooden or leather soles. The person used thin strips of leather to hold the soles on the feet.

Make a pair of sandals. Have the child place his feet on a piece of leather. Trace around each foot. Cut out the patterns. Make holes around the edges. Lace leather thongs through the holes. Tie thongs around the ankles. The sandals can be used for Bible plays or for wearing at casual times to see how shoes felt that were worn long ago.

NEW TO ME

It is true that there is no new thing under the sun. God put everything here that we need to use. However, we can put those materials together in unique ways to create gadgets to make life easier or more interesting. Have the children design gadgets that will help them. For example, they might invent a gadget to guarantee that they would say their prayers each night. Have them draw pictures of the gadgets. Underneath, the students might explain how they work.

MY GADGET

At 8:30 every night, my robot would be programmed to stand by my bed. It would read me a Bible story. It would tell me to pray. If my prayer was recorded on its tape, it would go to the corner of the room. If I fell asleep without saying a prayer, it would buzz loudly every five minutes until I prayed.

PLAY A NEW TESTAMENT GAME

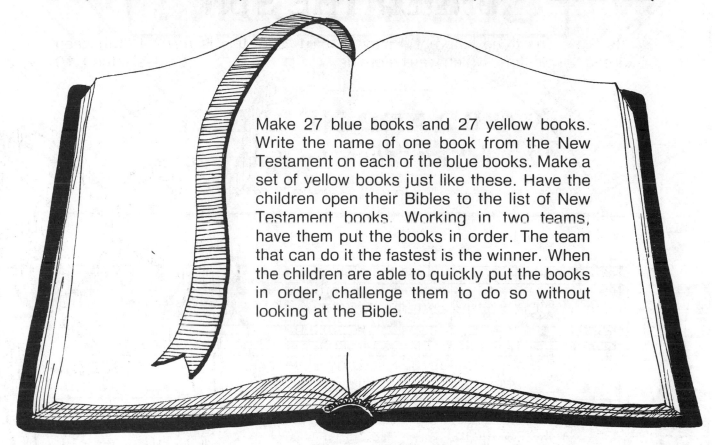

Make 27 blue books and 27 yellow books. Write the name of one book from the New Testament on each of the blue books. Make a set of yellow books just like these. Have the children open their Bibles to the list of New Testament books. Working in two teams, have them put the books in order. The team that can do it the fastest is the winner. When the children are able to quickly put the books in order, challenge them to do so without looking at the Bible.

A NEW COMMANDMENT FOR YOUR LIFE

Jesus gave His disciples a new commandment. This commandment will make a good pattern for the lives of the children. Have them memorize it and use it every day.

"A new commandment I give unto you, That ye love one another; as I have loved you, that ye also love one another."   John 13:34

NEW COMMANDMENT AWARD

_____ has memorized the new commandment

that Jesus gave in John 13:34. The commandment was used

when _____ showed love to _____

by _____

_____

_____

Signature

SEE ME SING!

A BRAND-NEW DAY
Words and Music by Kathy Jones

Rainbows, Dreams and Butterfly Wings, Copyright © 1984, Good Apple, Inc., Box 299, Carthage, IL 62321-0299

THE FIRST MIRACLE

A Pantomime

John 2:1-11

CHARACTERS

Jesus	Mary
Servants	Wedding Guests

Setting: A Jewish home—the wedding guests are milling around the room. Each guest has an empty glass in his hand. The servants are standing by the water jugs. Mary is by Jesus.

Guests: (Go to the water jugs where the servants are standing to ask for more to drink.)

Servants: (Tip over the water jugs to show that they are empty. They lift their hands to show there is no more. They shake their heads to show they are sorry.)

Mary: (Takes Jesus over to the water jugs. She tips one over so Jesus can see inside. She places the jug upright again and looks at Jesus in a pleading way as if asking Him to please take care of it.)

Jesus: (Looks in the jug when Mary tips it. Places His hand beside His head as if to think. Looks up to God to pray. Nods His head yes.)

Mary: (Talks to the servants while pointing to Jesus to show that the servants should do what Jesus tells them.)

Jesus: (Points to the water jugs and then off to the side to show that the servants should go to the well to get more water to fill the jugs.)

Servants: (Each runs off with a container in his hands to get water from the well. Each makes several trips each time pouring the water into the big jugs. When the jugs are full, each servant stands back and wipes his brow as if he has been working hard.)

Jesus: (Goes to the water jugs and looks up to heaven. He touches them and slightly tips one over. He then invites the servants to pour it for the guests.)

Guests: (All come to the water jugs to have the servants fill their glasses. They all smile after they take a taste to show that this is really good wine.)

GOD'S WINTER WONDERLAND

"HE GIVETH SNOW LIKE WOOL: HE SCATTERETH THE HOARFROST LIKE ASHES."
PSALM 147:16

Treasured moments are spent outside;
Bundled up we're ready to skate or slide.
I'm glad God used His gentle hand
To make a winter wonderland.

Back the bulletin board with blue paper. Draw in snowcapped mountains. Have the children write four-lined poems about winter on the snowballs. Have them illustrate their poems. Place these on the bulletin board.

WHAT IS COLD?

For a group activity, ask the children to match the line you give them about COLD. It should have the same number of syllables and it should rhyme.

COLD IS . . .
icy toes
runny nose

COLD IS . . .
lost mitten
frostbitten

CELEBRATE SNOWY DAYS

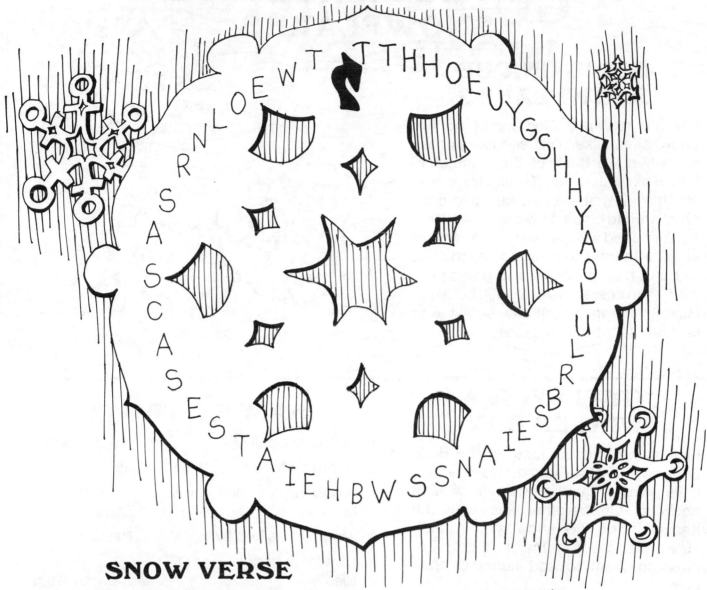

SNOW VERSE

Start at the arrow. Go around the snowball skipping every other letter. Find the Bible snow verse from Isaiah 1:18.

MAKE A SNOW SHAKE

Place one tray of ice cubes in an ice crusher. Crush the ice until it looks like snow. Pour it into a blender. Add ⅔ cup powdered milk, 2 tablespoons honey, and blend well. Pour into a tall glass and enjoy.

LION IN THE SNOW

Benaiah was a very brave man. He accomplished some extraordinary feats. He was so valiant that David made him head of his bodyguard. Read about his snowy adventure in II Samuel 23:20.

Answer to snow verse: Though your sins be as scarlet, they shall be as white as snow.

GOD MADE SNOWFLAKES

GOD'S UNIQUE SNOWFLAKES

We are told that God made no two snowflakes alike. This seems impossible when we think of the number of snowflakes that fall. To illustrate how much variety there can be, give each child a white circle. Have him fold it into a pie-shaped wedge, and make random snips with the scissors. Ask each child to open his snowflake and compare it with the others. No two will be alike. Have children mount the snowflakes on blue construction paper.

TRIVIA FOR A WINTER DAY

Find some unusual facts in the Bible and make a trivia game. Make snowballs. Write a fact on one side of each snowball. On the other side, write the answer. Cut the snowballs in half. Have the children match them. Encourage them to add items of their own.

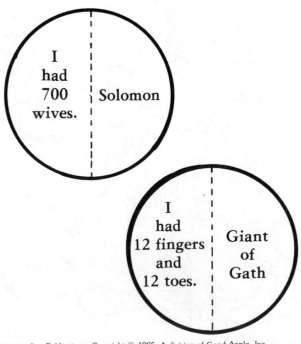

SAMPLE TRIVIA

1.	I lived to be 969.	Methuselah
2.	I used a stone for a pillow.	Jacob
3.	I was hairy when I was born.	Esau
4.	A donkey talked to me.	Balaam
5.	I had 12 fingers and 12 toes.	Giant of Gath
6.	I had 700 wives.	Solomon
7.	I had 88 children.	Rehoboam
8.	God allowed me to live 15 years longer.	Hezekiah
9.	I ate locusts.	John the Baptist
10.	I stole my father's idols.	Rachel
11.	I won a beauty contest.	Esther
12.	I won a battle with trumpets and torches.	Gideon
13.	This is the shortest verse in the Bible.	John 11:35
14.	This is the middle verse in the Bible.	Psalm 118:8

PUPPY FUN

Make a puppy calendar to record the antics of the puppy during the year.

PUPPY WANTED

Have each child who does not have a puppy write a want-ad for the special kind of puppy he would like to have. An example follows:

Wanted
A soft brown and white spotted puppy with bright shiny eyes. Must love to romp and play with a six-year-old boy.

JENNIFER IS MY GIRL

Discuss what the puppy does for the children. Have the children write stories from the viewpoint of the puppy.

Jennifer Is My Girl
In the morning I rush in and jump on Jennifer's bed to wake her up so she will not be late for school. I nibble on her ears and lick her cheek to show I love her. When she wants to play, I am always ready. When my girl needs a friend, she always comes to me. I listen to her and try to cheer her up when she is sad. Having a girl is a lot of work, but I love her so I do my job the best I can.

PUPPY AWARD

_____

took good care of the puppy this month by feeding it at just the right times. The puppy was played with often.

_____

is a good puppy owner.

_____
Signature

PUPPY TALK

DON MITCHELL

Verse One

I have this lit-tle pup-py dog; I love him ver-y much. He wags his tail when I come home; He snug-gles to my touch. We have these con-ver-sa-tions___ He talks with-out a word, And when I whis-per in his ear, His tail tells me he heard.

Chorus

I talk to my pup-py___ My pup-py talks to me; I know when he is sad or glad or when he needs a hug from me... He is my pup-py, he loves me 'cuz I'm me, And talk-ing to my lit-tle pup-py means an aw-ful lot to me.

Some people try to tell me a puppy can't talk back,
But they don't know my puppy; they haven't caught his act.
He tells me when he's angry; He tells me when he's sad.
Although he never talks out loud, he wiggles when he's glad.
Chorus:

My puppy is my buddy no matter what I do—
He loves me when I'm happy and when I'm sad and blue.
Thru thick 'n thin he's with me; he'll love me to the end,
I have to say without a doubt my puppy's my best friend.
Chorus:

FEBRUARY

1	2	3	4	5	6	7
Read I John 3:18.	Find a friend who has a February birthday.	Tell your mother how much you love her.	Ask your parents to read the story of Ruth to you.	Thank God for the Bible.	Find out about our tenth President.	Have a Bible birthday party.
8	**9**	**10**	**11**	**12**	**13**	**14**
Draw a baby eagle.	Make a valentine for your grandparents.	Make some heart-shaped cookies.	Send your Sunday School teacher a valentine.	Read a story about Honest Abe Lincoln.	Serve God with all your heart today.	Show love to your neighbor.
15	**16**	**17**	**18**	**19**	**20**	**21**
Thank God for loving you.	Find out about our national bird.	Thank God for our country.	Be loving to everyone today.	Pray for our President.	Find out about the White House.	Read a story about George Washington.
22	**23**	**24**	**25**	**26**	**27**	**28**
Pray that more people will love God.	Read John 3:16.	Find out about our fourth President.	Draw a picture showing ways you were loving this month.	Read I Corinthians 13.	Tell your dad how much you love him.	Show love to your brothers and/or sisters.

President's Day **16-19**
Patriotism Week **20-22**
Happy Birthday **23-24**
Valentine's Day **25-26**

PRESIDENT'S DAY

CELEBRATE PRESIDENT'S DAY

"Blessed is the nation whose God is the Lord . . . ."
Psalm 33:12

In Bible times, the leaders also went through a special ceremony. Often it was not public like the inauguration of our President. When Samuel anointed David to be king over Israel, only his family members were present. Samuel took a flask with oil and poured it on David. They prayed and the Spirit of God came on David. Place a small amount of mineral oil on each child's head. Pray with them so they can better understand the Biblical anointing of leaders.

Every four years in the month of January, a person stands on the steps of the Capitol in Washington, D.C., to take the oath of the President. In this ceremony, the person places the left hand on an open Bible. The right hand is upraised. The Presidential Oath is then repeated: "I do solemnly swear (or affirm) that I will faithfully execute the Office of the President of the United States and will, to the best of my ability, preserve, protect, and defend the Constitution of the United States."

Discuss the meaning of this oath. Have the children go through the process so they can understand what the President does on this special day.

"Open ye the gates, that the righteous nation which keepeth the truth may enter in."
Isaiah 26:2

MEET OUR LEADERS

GEORGE WASHINGTON

When our first President, George Washington, was a schoolboy, he copied rules of behavior in his exercise book. Here are some of his rules:

Turn not your back to others, especially in speaking.

Jog not the table on which another reads or writes.

Be not curious to know the affairs of others.

While you are talking, point not your finger.

Keep your fingers neat and clean at the table and when foul wipe them on a corner of your table napkin.

Add some good behavior rules to the ones George Washington wrote.

JIMMY CARTER

Jimmy Carter decided to try to sell some peanuts from his father's farm when he was only six years old. He dug the vines and loaded them into his wagon. At home he soaked the peanuts overnight and then boiled them in salt water. He put the peanuts in bags and walked into Plains, Georgia, to sell them. Jimmy still thinks that boiled peanuts are better than roasted ones. Purchase some raw peanuts. Soak them overnight. Boil them in salt water.

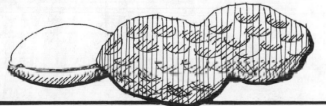

JESUS CHRIST

When Jesus was a little boy, His mother taught Him God's laws. When Jesus grew up, He showed the people how to live better lives. Here are some ways Jesus showed how to live a better life:

Love God with all your heart.

Love your neighbor.

Be kind to your enemies.

Take care of poor people who cannot provide for themselves.

Obey your parents.

Forgive people who wrong you.

Learn the song "The Things Jesus Taught Us" by Kathy Jones. It is on the next page.

MOSES

God gave Moses a tremendous job to do. He was to lead the people out of Egypt because they had been made slaves there. After Moses rescued the people, he led them out into the desert. God provided manna for them. The people got tired of eating the same thing. They wanted some variety.

Write a recipe showing how you would use manna. Put your recipes together to make a manna cookbook.

THE THINGS JESUS TAUGHT US

Words and Music
by
Kathy Jones
Lakewood, CA

LET'S BE FREE

GEORGE WASHINGTON CARVER

George Washington Carver was a slave who had been set free. He was a very intelligent Black man and became a botanist. He was especially interested in inventing ways to use peanuts. He thought of over three hundred uses. See how many ways you can think of to use a peanut.

Peanut Butter Balls

Mix together:
½ cup wheat germ
1 cup sunflower seeds
½ cup coconut
½ cup raisins
½ cup sesame seeds
1½ cups oatmeal

Add:
½ cup honey
1½ cups peanut butter

Mix thoroughly. Shape into balls. Enjoy!

ABRAHAM LINCOLN

Abraham Lincoln was known as the President who freed the slaves. The Emancipation Proclamation declared that slaves were to be freed in the Confederate States. Although the slaves were not freed immediately, progress was made in that direction. Make a list of reasons why it would not be pleasant to be a slave.

SLAVERY IN BIBLE TIMES

Slavery was not encouraged for the Jews, but it was permitted in Bible times. The Israelites were slaves to the Egyptians. Sometimes they were not treated kindly. The law that was given to Moses protected the slaves. They were to have certain privileges:

They were to rest on the Sabbath.

They were to join in the religious festivals.

They were not to be injured by their masters.

If they suffered injury, they were to be set free.

The masters were to be kind to the slaves. Most of the slaves held by the Jews were people they had captured in battles with other nations. A Hebrew could become a slave. However, he could serve his master for only six years. After that he was to be set free. The master was to give him some animals and provide him with food until he could earn some of his own.

Make a diorama showing a slave leaving his master. Make sure he has plenty of supplies.

PATRIOTISM WEEK

SEALS OF LEADERSHIP

This is the Great Seal of the United States. The eagle is our national bird. It is holding olive branches, which stand for peace. The arrows mean that we will fight to defend our country and our freedom. At the beginning of our country, there were only thirteen colonies. Later these were made states. The number *thirteen* is used for many things in our country. See how many thirteens can be found on the Great Seal.

Design your own seal. Try to depict characteristics that are typical of you. If you are loving, you could draw a heart with hands going out from it. Use your imagination!

Seals were used by leaders whom we read about in the Bible. Sometimes the king's seal was used to carry out misdeeds. Jezebel wanted her husband, King Ahab, to have Naboth's vineyard. Naboth did not want to sell his land. This made Jezebel very angry. She wrote letters in Ahab's name and put his seal on them. She wanted people to tell lies about Naboth so she could put him to death. The people did as she requested. Poor Naboth was stoned to death. Ahab and Jezebel took Naboth's land after he was dead.

AHAB

Another king's seal was used to write a proclamation that would cause all of the Jews to be killed. Read about this seal in the book of Esther.

The Holy Spirit puts His seal on us when we believe. This is a very beautiful seal.

Shining Star Publications, Copyright © 1985, A division of Good Apple, Inc.

OUR NATIONAL BIRD

Duplicate the eagle on cardstock so every child has one. Have each child cut out a bird and glue on the items as suggested. Spray the entire bird with gold paint. Back the eagles with red or blue construction paper. Place them on the bulletin board.

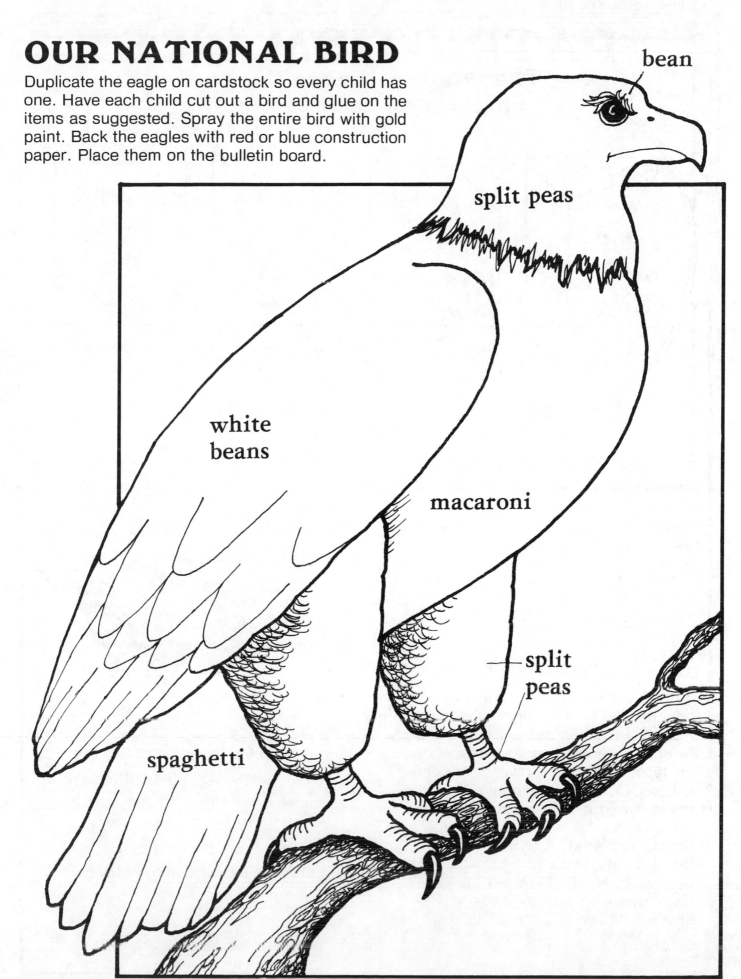

bean

split peas

white beans

macaroni

split peas

spaghetti

They that wait upon the Lord shall renew their strength.

They shall mount up with wings as eagles.

Using the pictures the children have made of eagles, construct the board above using blue background paper.

THE DOVE

Just as the eagle is the symbol of our country, the dove is the symbol of the Holy Spirit. When Jesus was baptized by John the Baptist, a dove descended on Jesus. A dove is known for its gentle actions. Doves were also used for sacrifices when people were too poor to bring lambs. Mary and Joseph brought two turtledoves as a sacrifice when they brought Jesus to the temple to be dedicated. Noah also used the gentle dove when he was in the ark. Read about this dove in Genesis 8:6-14.

I WILL SOAR LIKE AN EAGLE

_____

has learned Isaiah 40:31: "But they that wait upon the Lord shall renew their strength; they shall mount up with wings as eagles; they shall run, and not be weary; and they shall walk, and not faint."

_____
Signature

HAPPY BIRTHDAY

MAKE BIRTHDAY BOOKS

Make birthday books so the children can remember how they celebrated their special days each year. For each book, you will need two pieces of poster board 6'' X 9'' for the front and back covers. Lay them down side by side leaving a small space between them. Place masking tape down the center.

Turn the cover over. Place masking tape down this side also. Fold ten pieces of typing paper in half. Place the fold in the center of the masking tape. With a large needle and thread, sew through the masking tape and the typing paper.

Starting this year, have each child write how he celebrated his birthday. Use the first full page. On the right side, have him write the story. On the left side, instruct him to draw a gift that he received. Next year another story and another picture can be added.

TELL ABOUT BIBLE BIRTHDAYS

PHARAOH'S BIRTHDAY

Genesis 40:20-22
On Pharaoh's birthday a huge feast was given. During the party, Pharaoh called for the butler and the baker, who had been in prison for a long time. The butler got his job back. The baker wasn't so fortunate. Pharaoh ordered him to be hanged.

HEROD'S BIRTHDAY

Matthew 14:6-12
At Herod's birthday party, a young girl's dancing pleased Herod so much that he told her he would give her anything she requested. She asked for John the Baptist to be killed. Herod was sorry, but he had made a promise, and he kept his word. John the Baptist was beheaded. This was not a very happy birthday party. Have the children tell what they would have asked for if the king said they could have anything they wanted.

LET'S HAVE A PARTY

Plan a special birthday party. Eat like the common people in Bible times.

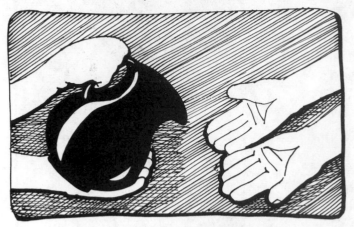

DIP WITH ME

No silverware was used. The people used thin bread to dip the food out of the bowls. The only dishes on the mat were the ones which contained the food. No individual dishes were used. Everyone dipped into the same bowls with their pieces of bread.

LET'S PRAY AGAIN

After the meal was over, everyone prayed to thank God for providing the meal.

PLEASE WASH YOUR HANDS

Washing the hands before eating was a very important custom for the Jews. To make sure their hands were clean, they had someone pour water over them after they were washed.

EVERYONE PRAY

Before starting to eat, each person repeated the prayer that the head of the house said.

NO TABLES ALLOWED

No tables or chairs were used. Instead, a mat was placed on the floor. The people sat around the mat with their legs folded under them.

WASH YOUR HANDS AGAIN

Since the fingers were used a great deal during the meal, it was necessary to wash them again. This time, also, they had someone pour water over them to make sure they were clean.

VALENTINE'S DAY

"My little children, let us not love in word, neither in tongue; but in deed and in truth."   I John 3:18

WE LOVE ONE ANOTHER

Make a Bible game of sweethearts. Cut eight red hearts and eight white hearts. On each red heart, write the name of a man. On each white heart, write the name of the woman he married. Match the couples.

Adam/Eve
David/Bath-sheba
Elkanah/Hannah
Jacob/Rachel
Abraham/Sarah
Isaac/Rebekah
Joseph/Mary
Boaz/Ruth

God created all things for us to enjoy. Make a love mobile showing the items the children most love that God made for them.

Thank You for Your Love

You showed love to me when . . . .

LOVE LETTERS

Send a love letter to each member of the family. Fold a red piece of paper in half from top to bottom. Cut a heart leaving the top fold uncut. On the outside write: "Thank You for Your Love." On the inside write how that person showed love for you. Deliver the cards on Valentine's Day.

LET US LOVE ONE ANOTHER

"... my cup runneth over. Surely goodness and mercy shall follow me all the days of my life ...." Psalm 23:5-6

Each time a child shows love, record it on a small heart. Drop the heart into the cup. See how long it takes for the cup to run over.

WHO IS MY NEIGHBOR?

Jesus told us to love our neighbors. To illustrate who our neighbors are, He told the parable of "The Good Samaritan." Read this parable in Luke 10:30-37. Do the pantomime from *Acting for God* by Kathy Jones (a Shining Star publication).

LEARN A LOVE VERSE

"Beloved, if God so loved us, we ought also to love one another."   I John 4:11

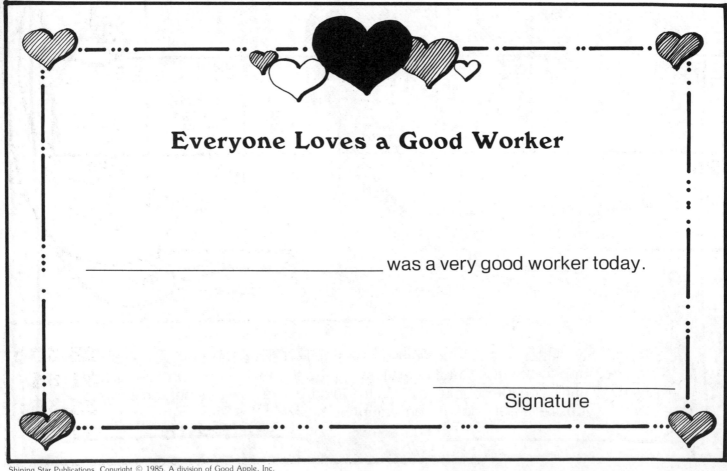

Everyone Loves a Good Worker

_____ was a very good worker today.

_____
Signature

MARCH

1 Celebrate World Day of Prayer.	**2** Begin recording the windy days.	**3** Learn Luke 11:9.				
4 Pray for your pastor.	**5** Make a sailboat.	**6** Draw a windy-day picture.	**7** Find out how God answered Hannah's prayer. I Sam. 2			
8 Pray for your parents.	**9** Read about the publican's prayer. Luke 18:10-14	**10** Make a weather vane.	**11** "Pray without ceasing." I Thess. 5:17	**12** Ask God to help you in school.		
13 Read about the windy parable in Matthew 7:24-27.	**14** Remember to say grace before meals.	**15** Learn the Lord's Prayer. Matthew 6	**16** Read about Paul's windy adventure. Acts 27	**17** Look for crocuses today.	**18** Pray for the people in your church.	
19 Read about Rhoda. Acts 12:13-19	**20** Find out what the wind did to Job's children. Job 1:19	**21** Enjoy the first day of spring.	**22** Start planting a garden.	**23** Tell someone about an answered prayer.	**24** Read about Naboth's garden. I Kings 21	**25** Pray for your family.
26 Find out what Jesus did in the Garden of Gethsemane.	**27** Tell a friend about the Garden of Eden.	**28** Water your garden.	**29** Read about a king's garden. Esther 1:5, 6	**30** Have your parents tell you the Parable of the Sower. Matthew 13	**31** Make a graph of the windy days this month.	

WORLD DAY OF PRAYER

TEACH CHILDREN TO PRAY

Use the bulletin board to teach the children the different kinds of prayer.

1. Prayer is worshiping God:
   ". . . Our Father which art in heaven, Hallowed be thy name." Matthew 6:9

2. Prayer is listening:
   "Thou wilt keep him in perfect peace, whose mind is stayed on thee . . . ." Isaiah 26:3

3. Prayer is confessing:
   "If we confess our sins, he is faithful and just to forgive us our sins . . . ." I John 1:9

4. Prayer is thanking God:
   "In every thing give thanks: for this is the will of God . . . ." I Thessalonians 5:18

5. Prayer is singing to God:
   "Serve the Lord with gladness: come before his presence with singing." Psalm 100:2

6. Prayer is talking to God:
   "Ask, and it shall be given you . . . ." Matthew 7:7

Have children pray sentence prayers using each of these different kinds of prayer.

Cover the board with blue butcher paper. Enlarge the figures and place on the board as shown.

PRAYER OPENS THE PRISON DOORS

Acts 12:5-19

CHARACTERS

Narrator   Rhoda
Peter   Angel
Friend 1   Friend 2
Two guards

Scene 1

Setting: House of Peter's friends—they are praying for Peter.

Narrator: After Jesus went back to heaven, His disciples were told to tell people about God's love. Some listened, but others hated the disciples. King Herod had already killed James, the brother of John, and now he had Peter put in prison. Peter's friends are praying for him.

Friend 1: Oh, Jesus, please save Peter. Don't let him be killed by King Herod.

Friend 2: (praying) Peter has been in prison for many days. Tomorrow, Herod is planning to kill him. Please, God, protect my friend.

Rhoda: (praying) Peter is my wonderful friend. He has told so many people about God's love. He taught me many things about God. Rescue my friend so he can tell more people about your love.

Scene 2

Setting: In a prison—Peter is half-asleep on the floor and chained to two guards.

Narrator: Meanwhile, Peter is half-asleep in prison. Suddenly something unusual happens.

Angel: Wake up, Peter. Get up quickly.

Peter: (The chains fall off.) Yes, sir. But who are you?

Angel: Never mind who I am. We must move quickly. Get dressed and put on your sandals.

Peter: Yes, sir. (He hurriedly dresses.)

Angel: Wrap your coat around yourself and follow me.

Peter: Where are we going?

Angel: You will see. You must be quiet now.

Narrator: Silently the angel and Peter walk past the guards and into the courtyard. Suddenly the large iron gate opens by itself. The two walk through the gate.

Scene 3

Setting: Walking along the street.

Angel: I will be able to walk with you for only a short time.

Peter: (walking) I can hardly believe that I am out of prison. Thank you. You saved my life. (The angel leaves quickly.)

Peter: (talking to himself) Where did he go? He must have been an angel. Yes, I am sure of it. God sent His angel to rescue me from prison. But where will I go? Where will I be safe? I must hurry. The people on the street may recognize me. I will go to Mary's house. I will be safe there.

Narrator: Peter walks quickly to Mary's house, the mother of John Mark. When he arrives, he hears people praying inside. He knocks loudly.

Scene 4

Setting: The house of Peter's friends.

Rhoda: Who is knocking so loudly?

Peter: It is Peter. God has rescued me from prison.

Rhoda: It can't be Peter. But it is! I recognize your voice. I must tell the others. (She runs back into the room.)

Rhoda: (excitedly) Come and see. Peter is at the door. He has escaped from prison. Come quickly!

Friend 1: Rhoda, you are not thinking clearly. Herod had double guards placed on Peter. He could not be at our door!

Rhoda: But he is! I heard his voice. No one speaks like Peter.

Friend 2: You are out of your mind, Rhoda. It can't be Peter. Maybe you are imagining that you are seeing his spirit. Herod would never release Peter.

Rhoda: Come and see! You will believe me then.

Peter: (knocks on the door again)

Rhoda: Come on. He is knocking again. (The friends go to the door.)

Friend 1: Peter! Is it really you? (Hugs him and tells him he is glad to see him.)

Friend 2: Peter, we have prayed for you to be rescued from prison, but I guess we didn't really believe God would do it. How glad I am to see you!

Narrator: Yes, Jesus had answered the prayers of Peter's friends. He rescued Peter so he could tell many more people about God's loving care.

WINDY DAYS

THE WINDY PARABLE

"Therefore everyone who hears these words of mine and *puts them into practice* is like a wise man who built his house on the rock. The rain came down, the streams rose, and the winds blew and beat against that house; yet it did not fall, because it had its foundation on the rock."   Matthew 7:24, 25(NIV)

Tell the story of the wise and foolish builders from Matthew 7. Emphasize that one must put into practice what is known about God's love. Have each child draw a house. Encourage him to discuss something he did to show God's love. If he can relate an incident, he should draw a rock under his house and write the incident on the rock. Make a bulletin board from the houses.

THE SMELLS OF WIND

Wind can bring us many smells. Good smells like bread baking in the oven—bad smells like food burning on the stove. Identify the smells the moving air is bringing to your classroom right now.

EAT A WINDY SNACK

Place a lettuce leaf on the plate. Place half a peach or pear on the lettuce with the hollow side up. To make the sail, roll a piece of white bread with a rolling pin until it is flat. Cut this into triangles. Place a toothpick through the sail. Anchor it in the boat.

THE WIND AND THE WAVES OBEY HIM

Jesus had preached to many people. He got into a boat and went sound asleep. Without warning, a storm came up on the lake. The disciples were terrified. They went over to Jesus and woke Him up. They said, ''Lord, save us or we are going to drown.'' Jesus told the disciples not to be afraid. He told the winds and the waves to stop. Immediately the weather was calm. The disciples wondered what kind of man this was that even the wind and the waves obeyed Him.

Matthew 8:23-27

Make a sequencing game using this story. Make the outside of the file folder as shown. Make sixteen small boats. Glue eight of them inside the folder. Number them. Write one of these statements on each of the remaining boats:

Jesus got into the boat and went to sleep.

A storm came up.

Waves swept over the boat.

The disciples were scared.

The disciples woke Jesus.

Jesus told the disciples not to be afraid.

Jesus told the wind and waves to be still.

The disciples wondered what kind of man Jesus was, for the winds obeyed Him.

Write the directions on the back of the folder.

Directions:

One person may play this game. Read the statements on the boats. Place them in the order in which they happened by putting each boat on the appropriately numbered boat inside the folder.

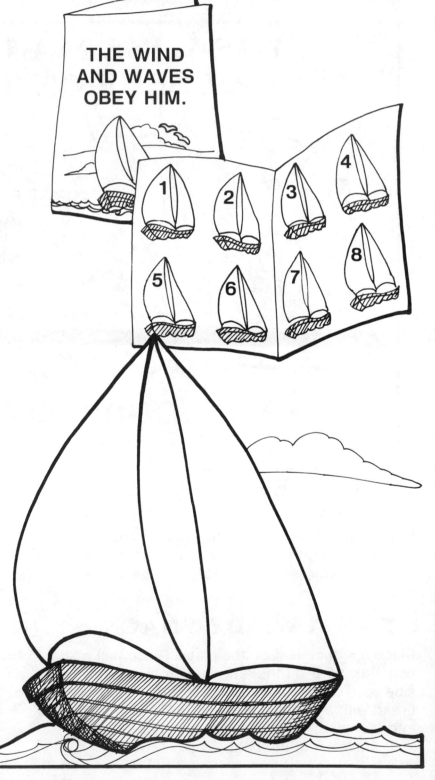

THE WIND AND WAVES OBEY HIM.

SAILING ON THE WINDY SEA

''A furious squall came up, and the waves broke over the boat. so that it was nearly swamped.''   Mark 4:37(NIV)

A squall is made up of many thunderstorms linked together. The winds in a squall are violent. Squalls happen when a strong wind blows over the top of a cold front. The hot air in front of the wind cannot rise to get out of the way. Shifting winds and heavy rain make squalls very dangerous. They move so fast that many small boats can be turned over very suddenly. Make an anemometer to see how fast the wind is blowing in your area.

You will need a block of wood, a dowel, a circle of poster board, four paper cups, and a nail. Glue the dowel in an upright position on the block of wood. Glue or staple the paper cups around the outside edges of the cardboard. A different color is needed for one of the cups. Painting it or marking it with a felt pen would make it easy to identify. Make a hole in the center of the cardboard. Pound the nail through the cardboard into the center of the dowel. Take your anemometer outside. By watching how many times the colored cup goes around, you can estimate how hard the wind is blowing.

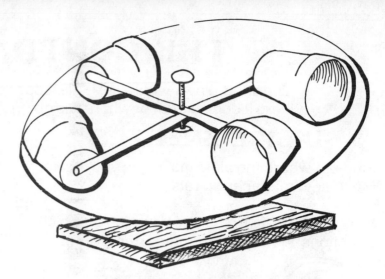

CATCH THE WIND

''. . . the centurion found an Alexandrian ship sailing for Italy and put us on board. We made slow headway for many days and had difficulty . . . . When the wind did not allow us to hold our course, we sailed to the lee of Crete . . . .''
                    Acts 27:6-7(NIV)

Sailboats were used in Bible times. Make a sailboat by shaping a piece of balsa wood. Glue a cloth or paper sail to a thin piece of metal. Attach the sail to the base. Sailboats cannot go directly into the wind. They must zigzag or ''tack'' to catch the wind. The sailor has to move the sails to catch the wind. Place the boat into a large pan of water on a windy day. Observe how the sailboat moves.

THE CONTRARY WINDS

"The wind blows wherever it pleases. You hear its sound, but you cannot tell where it comes from or where it is going . . . ."   John 3:8(NIV)

INSIDE BREEZES

Find out where the air is moving in your room. Make several paper spirals.

Hang the spirals from the ceiling to see which directions the currents of air are moving.

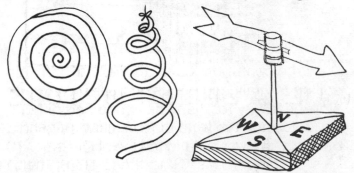

Winds can change directions quickly. Make a weather vane using a block of wood, a dowel, paint, cardboard, and a small plastic medicine bottle. Paint the block of wood with four different colors. Section it off as shown. Glue the dowel to the center of the block. Cut an arrow from the cardboard. Fasten the medicine bottle on one side of the arrow. Place the bottle over the dowel to help the arrow move freely. Place the weather vane outside and observe wind direction.

WINDY CINQUAINS

Write cinquains about the wind.

First line	One word
Second line	Two adjectives
Third line	Three verbs
Fourth line	Four words
Fifth line	Synonym for the first word

WIND
SOFT   GENTLE
WHISPERS   GLIDES   MOVES
PILES OF LEAVES RUSTLE
BREEZE

WIND
BLUSTERY   DANGEROUS
MOANS   HOWLS   SCREECHES
BLOWS SHIPS OFF COURSE
HURRICANE

"When a gentle south wind began to blow, they thought they had obtained what they wanted; so they weighed anchor . . . . Before very long, a wind of hurricane force, called the "Northeaster," swept down from the island. The ship was caught by the storm . . . ."
Acts 27:13-15(NIV)

FIRST DAY OF SPRING

OUR ORDERLY CREATION

God planned our earth perfectly. He wanted us to enjoy seasons. He tilted the earth so that different parts would be toward the sun. Make seasonal charts to show the differences in the times of the year.

Use pictures from magazines to show:
     appearances of plants during each season
     differences in clothing for each season
     differences in activities for each season

MAKE A SPRING PICTURE

Cut a colorful vase from construction paper. Draw limbs coming out of the vase. Snip small pieces of cotton balls. Glue these along the limbs to make pussy willows.

WRITE SPRING HAIKU

Haiku is a Japanese poetry form containing three lines about nature.

First line   5 syllables
Second line   7 syllables
Third line   5 syllables

Beautiful flowers
Rise up from the muddy ground
Fragrance is lovely

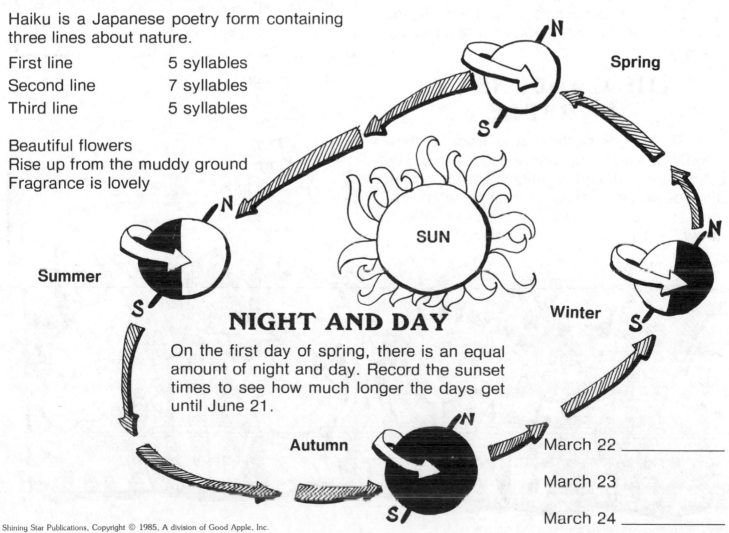

NIGHT AND DAY

On the first day of spring, there is an equal amount of night and day. Record the sunset times to see how much longer the days get until June 21.

March 22 _____

March 23 _____

March 24 _____

PLANT YOUR GARDEN

"And the Lord God planted a garden eastward in Eden; and there he put the man whom he had formed."
Genesis 2:8

Plant some radish seeds in an aluminum foil pan. Water them and they will soon be ready to eat.

THE PERFECT GARDEN

Write a story about the perfect garden where there are no weeds or harmful bugs. The moisture is just right. There are no strong winds or hail to cause damage. The only place where this could have happened is in the Garden of Eden.

Make a crayon resist picture of the perfect garden. Have the children draw and color very heavily the items they think would have been in the Garden of Eden. Go over the picture with thin green tempera paint. Be sure to go over the picture only once with the tempera paint or the crayon will not be able to resist it.

THE GARDENER'S PARABLE

Tell the Parable of the Sower from Matthew 13. Demonstrate the different kinds of soil by using a large diorama. Have the children plant the seeds. Draw pictures to show what happens to each seed. Beside each kind of soil, draw the type of person it represents.

Do a word search to find some foods that are mentioned in the Bible. These are written either vertically or horizontally.

A	L	M	O	N	D	S	C	H	O
P	A	C	E	G	M	N	U	T	N
P	O	L	I	V	E	I	C	O	I
L	E	N	T	I	L	S	U	N	O
E	G	C	J	L	O	N	M	W	N
S	R	O	D	B	N	K	B	H	B
B	A	R	L	E	Y	L	E	E	K
M	P	N	H	A	Y	O	R	A	F
P	E	M	A	N	N	A	Q	T	R

Almond   Lentils
Apples   Manna
Barley   Melon
Bean   Nut
Corn   Olive
Cucumber   Onion
Grape   Wheat
Leek

HOORAY! I LOST MY TOOTH

MAKE A TOOTH PILLOW

Cut two 9'' X 9'' squares from felt. Make a pocket by cutting a 2'' X 2'' square. Using fabric glue, attach the pocket to one of the 9-inch squares. Cut a triangle. Glue it just above the top of the 2-inch square. Attach lace to one 9-inch square. Allow the glue to dry. Place glue on three sides of the square. Place the other piece on top. Stuff with polyester batting. Glue the remaining side.

TOOTH DIARY

Make a tooth diary. Cut two tooth-shaped covers from white poster board. Insert ten sheets between the covers. Punch holes in the top. Tie with white yarn. Each time a child loses a tooth, another page in the diary may be filled in.

Diary Pages

I lost my _____

tooth on _____

I was at _____

when it came loose. I took

care of it by _____

_____

FOR SAFE KEEPING

Make a container to use for keeping the little teeth. Cut two teeth from white felt using the above pattern. Glue around the bottom and sides with white glue. Leave the top open. Place the child's tooth in the container.

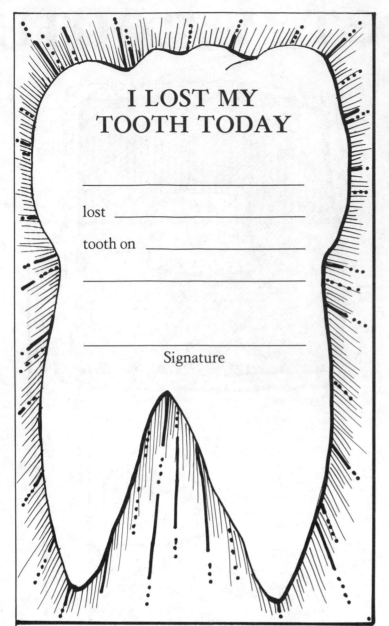

I LOST MY TOOTH TODAY

_____

lost _____

tooth on _____

_____

Signature

TOOTHY PUPPET

Make a tooth-shaped puppet from a paper bag. Place the top part of the face on the bottom of the bag. Place the bottom part of the mouth just under the crease in the bag. Slip a hand into it. Move the bottom part. It will appear as if the tooth is talking. Have the children explain how they will take care of their teeth using the puppet to tell the story.

DID YOU KNOW . . . .

''. . . I am escaped with the skin of my teeth'' is a quotation from the Bible?

Read why Job made this statement in Job 19. In spite of all of Job's troubles, he still loved God. Memorize Job 19:25.

TOOTH PICTOGRAPH

January	⊓ ∫
February	∫ ⊓
March	⊓ ⊓ ⊓

Each month display a new tooth. Write the names of the children who lose teeth in that month. Make a pictograph showing the numbers of teeth lost each month.

APRIL

1	2	3	4	5	6
Find out how the Garden of Eden was watered. Genesis 2:6	Start a chart of rainy days.	Read about Elijah's rainy story. I Kings 17-18	Have your parents tell you about the first rain.	Read Proverbs 28:3.	Look for a rainbow.
7	**8**	**9**	**10**	**11**	**12**
Write a rainbow poem.	Find out about God's water cycle.	Read how Johnny Apple-seed planted trees.	Celebrate Arbor Day.	Plant a new tree in your yard.	Find out about the forbidden tree. Genesis 2:9
13	**14**	**15**	**16**	**17**	**18**
Read about the day God made trees. Genesis 1:10-13	Do a play about Palm Sunday.	Celebrate Palm Sunday.	Read about the Passover. Exodus 12	Have a Passover Feast.	Tell your best friend the Passover story.
19	**20**	**21**	**22**	**23**	**24**
Share some charoseth (ground apples and nuts) with your friend.	Celebrate Good Friday.	Paint a Good Friday picture.	Celebrate Easter.	Write an Easter poem.	Tell some reasons you are glad that Jesus is alive.
25	**26**	**27**	**28**	**29**	**30**
Give an Easter lily to a shut-in.	Make an Easter banner.	Find out about the Emmaus walk. Luke 24	Count the rainy days this month.	Thank God for the resurrection of Jesus.	Draw a picture of a rainbow.

Shining Star Publications, Copyright © 1985, A division of Good Apple, Inc.

CELEBRATE ARBOR DAY

"If ye walk in my statutes, and keep my commandments, and do them; Then I will give you rain in due season, and the land shall yield her increase, and the trees of the field shall yield their fruit."
Leviticus 26:3, 4

When J. Sterling Morton moved from Detroit to Nebraska in 1854, he was dismayed because there were so few trees in that state. He was editor of the newspaper. He wrote articles encouraging people to plant trees. Arbor Day was first celebrated on April 10, 1872. A million trees were planted on this day. Celebrate Arbor Day this year by planting a tree either at school or at a church.

VALUABLE TREES

Trees were very valuable in Bible times, as they are today. When the Israelites were making war on a city, they were forbidden to destroy the trees ". . . for the tree of the field is man's life . . . ."
Deuteronomy 20:19

Survey the many uses we make of trees. Tell about the uses in Bible times:

Abraham used a tree for shade for his visitors (Genesis 18:4).

Hiram gave King Solomon cedar trees and fir trees to build the temple (I Kings 5:10).

Isaiah tells us the people used to burn trees for fuel (Isaiah 44:15).

Isaiah also reports that the people used trees to make idols (Isaiah 44:15).

Make a list of ways wood is used in our homes.

OUR LIVES ARE LIKE TREES

". . . every good tree bears good fruit, but a bad tree bears bad fruit . . . by their fruit you will recognize them." Matthew 7:17-20(NIV)

Draw trees showing the kinds of fruit the children are bearing in their lives.

ARBOR DAY AWARD

". . . he shall be like a tree planted by the rivers of water . . . ." Psalm 1:3

_____

helped to plant a _____

tree today.

_____

will help to take care of the tree by _____

_____

_____
Signature

WHAT KIND OF TREE . . .

1. did Jeremiah see when God was talking to him? Jeremiah 1:11 _____

2. did Jesus see Nathanael standing by before He called him to be His disciple? John 1:48 _____

3. did Solomon have carved on the walls of the temple? I Kings 6:29 _____

4. did Solomon use to cover the floor of the temple? I Kings 6:15 (two kinds) _____, _____

5. did Absalom get his hair caught in while he was riding his mule? II Samuel 18:9 _____

6. did the dove find when it was sent out from Noah's ark? Genesis 8:11 _____

7. did the people take branches from to greet Jesus as He came into Jerusalem? John 12:13 _____

8. did the Israelites use to build their booths for the Feast of Tabernacles? Nehemiah 8:15 (four kinds) _____, _____, _____, _____

9. did the angel sit under when he appeared to Gideon? Judges 6:11 _____

10. did Elijah sit down under after he was tired from running away from Jezebel? I Kings 19:4, 5 _____

11. did God use to help David know when to fight the Philistines? II Samuel 5:24 _____

12. did Hiram give to Solomon? I Kings 5:10 (two kinds) _____, _____

13. did King David use in building his own house? II Samuel 7:2 _____

14. did Jesus cause to die because it had no fruit? Mark 11:20 _____

15. did Adam and Eve take leaves from to make clothes for themselves? Genesis 3:7 _____

16. did Jacob use to make rods to place in front of the cattle watering troughs? Genesis 30:37 (three kinds) _____, _____, _____

JUNIPER
ALMOND OLIVE
PINE FIG OAK
POPLAR HAZEL PALM
FIR CHESTNUT CEDAR
MULBERRY
MYRTLE

Answers:
1. almond 2. fig 3. palm
4. fir, cedar 5. oak 6. olive
7. palm 8. olive, pine, myrtle palm
9. oak 10. juniper
11. mulberry 12. cedar, fir
13. cedar 14. fig 15. fig
16. poplar, hazel, chestnut

PASSOVER

The Passover had its beginning in the story told in Exodus 12. The Israelites were told to eat a roasted lamb and put the blood on the two side posts and on the upper doorposts of their houses. They were to eat unleavened bread and bitter herbs. The death angel would kill all of the firstborn in Egypt who did not have the blood on the doorposts. The death angel would ''pass over'' all those who had followed that direction. Celebrate the Passover as it may have been observed in the time of Jesus.

1. A platter of lamb is set in the center of the table. Around it sits bitter herbs, salt water, charoseth (ground apples and nuts) and grape juice.

2. The host prays thanking God for the fruit of the vine. (Drink the grape juice.)

3. The host then washes his hands. He dips the bitter herbs (lettuce and parsley) into the salt water. This is passed around for everyone to dip into the salt water.

4. The remaining food is removed from the table.

5. The host pours another glass of grape juice but does not drink it yet.

6. The youngest person asks these questions: Why is this night different from other nights? Why do we eat only unleavened bread tonight? Why do we eat only bitter herbs tonight? Why do we dip twice? Why must we have only roasted meat?

7. The host tells the story to answer the child's questions. The food is returned to the table. Psalms 113, 114 are read.

8. They drink the second cup of grape juice.

9. They wash their hands and eat after two blessings are asked on the food. The host dips the bread he has broken into the bitter herbs and the sweet charoseth. He gives this to each person. The lamb is then eaten. A third cup of grape juice is poured and everyone drinks it.

10. A blessing is said.

11. They recite Psalms 115-118. They drink a fourth cup of grape juice.

12. They sing a song.

13. The feast is over.

PALM SUNDAY

THE LORD NEEDS THEM

". . . Go to the village ahead of you, and at once you will find a donkey tied there, with her colt by her. Untie them and bring them to me."   Matthew 21:2(NIV)

When Jesus told His disciples to get a donkey, He also told them what to say if someone asked why they were taking it. They were to say that the Lord needs it.

Tell the story of the Triumphal Entry into Jerusalem from Matthew 21. Have the children write a story about how the owner of the donkey felt when he found out how his donkey was used that day.

HOSANNA TO THE HIGHEST

"They took palm branches and went out to meet him, shouting, 'Hosanna! Blessed is he who comes in the name of the Lord'. . . ."
                    John 12:13(NIV)

Lay palm leaves on green construction paper. Using a small sponge dipped into white tempera paint, dab white paint all over the paper. Allow it to dry for a short time. Lift the palm branches off the paper.

CONCENTRATE ON PALM SUNDAY

Make nine 2'' X 3'' green cards and nine yellow cards. Write a question on each green card and the answer on each yellow card. Place them face down with the green cards on the left and the yellow cards on the right. Two children may play this game. The players take turns trying to match a question with its answer. The winner is the child who finds the most correct matches.

1. What animal did Jesus ride?	Donkey
2. What city did Jesus visit?	Jerusalem
3. How many disciples were sent to get the animal?	Two
4. What message did the crowd shout?	Hosanna to the Son of David
5. What items did people place in the path?	Garments and palm branches
6. What question did the people ask?	Who is this man?
7. Who rode the donkey?	Jesus
8. What were the disciples to say if someone asked them about the donkey?	The Lord needs it.
9. Where were the disciples to find the donkey?	In the village

WRITE GOOD FRIDAY COUPLETS

A couplet is a two-line poem in which the last words in the lines rhyme.

Jesus died for you and me
Upon the cruel Calvary's tree.

GOOD FRIDAY

Have a mock trial. You (the teacher) read the sections while assigned children act out the trial. Use Matthew 26:57-68 and Matthew 27:11-31.

GOOD FRIDAY ART

"Then were there two thieves crucified with him, one on the right hand, and another on the left."   Matthew 27:38

Give each child a 9" X 12" sheet of white paper. Give the children the following directions: Go over the paper with a wide brush dipped in water. Make it wet, but do not leave puddles. Dip the brush in red water color. Go across the top of the paper. Alternate down the paper using yellow, orange, and purple. The color should be light. Allow the paper to dry. Using charcoal, draw in three large crosses.

JESUS DIED FOR ALL THE WORLD

MAKE AN EASTER BANNER

Supply a 12" X 18" piece of felt, a 14" dowel, scraps of felt, and patterns for tracing letters. Have the children design an Easter banner. These may be displayed around the room.

BETRAYED FOR 30 PIECES OF SILVER

Matthew 26:14-56

To make a file folder game, cut 30 circles from aluminum foil. Glue 15 circles on each side of the interior of the folder. Make question cards with dots to indicate how many circles the child may cover if a correct answer is given. Supply 30 circles to place over the foil circles.

One reader and two players are needed for this game. Each player takes one side of the folder. The reader gives a question to the first player. If he answers correctly, he may cover that number of spaces on the folder. If he answers incorrectly, the question is placed at the bottom of the stack and the other player is given a question. The winner is the first one to cover all his circles.

QUESTIONS

1. For how much did Judas agree to betray Jesus? (30 pieces of silver) ● ●

2. Who gave Judas the money? (The chief priests) ● ●

3. When Jesus said one of them would betray Him, what question did the disciples ask? (Is it I?) ● ● ●

4. How would the disciples know which one would betray Jesus? (He would dip his hand in the dish with Jesus.) ● ● ●

5. How did Jesus answer Judas when he asked, ''Is it I?'' (''Thou hast said.''—or yes) ● ● ●

6. Where did Jesus go to pray? (Garden of Gethsemane) ● ● ●

7. Where did Judas sit at the Passover Feast? (Next to Jesus) ● ● ●

8. How did the disciples feel when Jesus said one of them would betray Him? (Sorrowful) ● ● ●

9. How many people were having supper together? (The 12 disciples and Jesus) ● ●

10. What weapons did the crowd have? (Swords and staves) ● ● ● ●

11. How did Judas betray Jesus? (With a kiss) ● ● ●

12. What happened to a man's ear? (Someone cut it off.) ● ● ● ●

13. What did Jesus do to the man's ear? (Healed it) ● ● ●

14. What did the disciples do when Jesus was arrested? (Ran away) ● ● ●

15. How long did Jesus ask the disciples to pray? (One hour) ● ● ● ●

IN THE GARDEN OF GETHSEMANE
(A Pantomime)
CHARACTERS

Jesus	12 Disciples
Judas	Soldiers

Setting: In the Garden of Gethsemane (Matthew 26:36-56)

Jesus and Disciples: (Walk to the garden. Jesus leaves 8 of them at one spot. He folds His hands to indicate He wants them to pray.)

Jesus, Peter, James and John: (Walk on a little ways. The disciples look very sad.)

Jesus: (Points to the ground and folds His hands as if asking them to pray. He holds up one finger to indicate He wants them to pray one hour. Walks on and kneels down to pray. He seems very concerned.)

Disciples: (Lie down and go to sleep.)

Jesus: (Walks back to the disciples and finds them sleeping. He shakes them to wake them. Again He folds His hands in a praying position.)

Disciples: (Get up sleepily and shake their heads to say yes.)

Jesus: (Goes back to pray.)

Disciples: (Go back to sleep after praying a short time.)

Jesus: (Comes back to find the disciples sleeping again. He wakes them and goes back to pray.)

Disciples: (Go back to sleep again.)

Jesus: (Comes back to check on the disciples again. Wakes them and helps them to get up.)

Judas and Soldiers: (Enter garden.)

Judas: (Runs over and kisses Jesus.)

Soldiers: (Seize Jesus.)

Peter: (Raises sword and cuts off a soldier's ear.)

Jesus: (Heals the soldier's ear by placing it back on his head. He looks disapprovingly at Peter.)

Soldiers: (Lead Jesus away.)

Disciples: (Run away.)

CELEBRATE EASTER

Read about the appearances of Jesus to these people. Have the children draw pictures of the appearances to the people. Place these on the bulletin board.

Mary Magdalene	Mark 16:9	Other women	Matthew 28:8, 9
Emmaus Road	Luke 24:13-15	Thomas	John 20:26-31
By the Sea of Galilee	John 21:1-25	Five Hundred	I Corinthians 15:6
Peter	Luke 24:34	James	I Corinthians 15:7

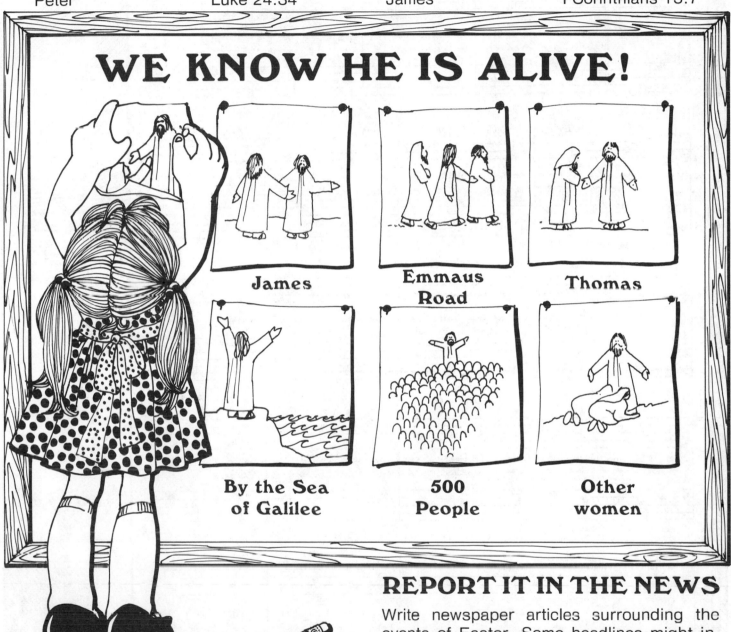

WE KNOW HE IS ALIVE!

James

Emmaus Road

Thomas

By the Sea of Galilee

500 People

Other women

WHEN WILL IT BE?

Calculate when Easter will be next year. It is always the first Sunday after the full moon following the first day of spring. Easter can never come before March twenty-second or after April twenty-fifth.

REPORT IT IN THE NEWS

Write newspaper articles surrounding the events of Easter. Some headlines might include:

Women Find Empty Tomb

Soldiers Report Earthquake

Chief Priests Bribe Soldiers

Emmaus Couple See Jesus

We Thought He Was a Ghost

Mystery Remains Unsolved

I Saw Him with My Own Eyes

I WONDER
Words and Music
by Kathy Jones

RAINY DAYS

"For yet seven days, and I will cause it to rain upon the earth forty days and forty nights . . . ."
Genesis 7:4

EVAPORATING A FLOOD

Read the story of the flood in Genesis 7 and 8. Notice the dates mentioned. Help the children to calculate how long it took for the puddles to dry out from the flood so Noah and his family could leave the ark.

ELIJAH PRAYED FOR RAIN

"Elijah . . . prayed earnestly that it would not rain, and it did not rain on the land for three and a half years. Again he prayed, and the heavens gave rain . . . ." James 5:17-18(NIV)

Read about Elijah's adventures with rain in I Kings 17:1-18:45.

Make a cloudy picture. Use cotton for clouds. Cut strips of crepe paper for the mountains. Place glue on the paper and push it into place with a pencil.

WHERE DO THE PUDDLES GO?

After it rains, there are puddles everywhere. To help explain where the puddles go, set a pan of water in the room. Watch it daily to see the water evaporate. To learn how heat affects evaporation, set one pan of water in the sun and another one inside the refrigerator. Record and compare the time it takes for the water to evaporate in each pan.

Many people believe that Noah saw the first rain. Prior to this time, a mist came up and watered the earth. The first rain must have been a shocking experience for those people outside the ark. Write limericks telling about the feelings of the people when they saw the rain. A limerick is a five-line poem. Lines one, two and five rhyme. Lines three and four also rhyme.

Raining down on us I see
Puddles growing immeasurably;
Men cry out
A lusty shout,
This will be the end of me.

HAVE A RAINBOW DAY
RAINBOW FEELINGS

The rainbow represents a promise God made to the people. A rainbow should make us feel very happy. Have the children describe their feelings when they see a rainbow.

Whenever I see a rainbow, I feel . . . .

MAKE A RAINBOW

Set a clear glass dish in a sunny window. Fill it with water. Lay a piece of white paper on the floor so the sun can shine through the bowl and onto the paper.

HOW BEAUTIFUL HEAVEN MUST BE

''. . . there was a rainbow round about the throne, in sight like unto an emerald.''

Revelation 4:3

Heaven is described in Revelation 4 as a very beautiful place. God wants all of us to go live with Him, but only those who have followed His plan of salvation will be allowed to view heaven. Explain God's plan to the children.

A RAINBOW DAY

_____ had a rainbow

day today because _____

_____

_____

Signature

''. . . the bow shall be in the cloud; and I will look upon it, that I may remember the everlasting covenant between God and every living creature of all flesh that is upon the earth.''

Genesis 9:16

MAY

1 Make a May basket.

2 Count the kinds of flowers in bloom.

3 Think about what Jesus said of the lilies. Matt. 6:28,29

4 What flower did Moses see? Exodus 2:3

5 Read Song of Solomon 2:1

6 Take a flower to your teacher.

7 Play "May I" with your friends.

8 Think about the values your mother taught you.

9 Find out what "honor" means.

10 Plan new ways to help your mother.

11 Learn Exodus 20:12

12 Make a carnation for Mother's Day.

13 Celebrate Mother's Day.

14 Find out about Sisera's mother. Judges 4-5

15 Read about the angel who visited Samson's mother. Judges 13

16 Have your parents tell you about Samuel's mother.

17 **18** Mom

19 Find what Elijah did for a special mother. I Kings 17

20 Read about Pentecost in Acts 2.

21 Learn about the Feast of Weeks. Exodus 34:22

22 Share some food with someone less fortunate.

23 Ask your parents about your ancestors.

24 Plan games for a family picnic.

25 Plan your Memorial Day menu.

26 Learn about your most famous ancestor.

27 Identify a Bible person you would like to remember.

28 Celebrate Memorial Day.

29 Write an obituary for a Bible person.

30 Design a tombstone for a Bible person.

31 List the good things that happened to you this month.

CELEBRATE MAY DAY

MAY FLOWERS

Children in America celebrate May Day by making May baskets and filling them with flowers. These are delivered secretly to friends. Make May baskets using the pattern given on page 53. Duplicate pattern onto construction paper. Cut basket out, and fold along dotted lines. Glue bottom flaps to square section to form base. Glue side flap to other side of basket. Attach the handle by gluing it to the sides of the basket. Fill the baskets with fresh flowers or handmade flowers (see directions below). These baskets may be given to shut-ins or special friends.

To make simple flowers, cut four small circles from crepe paper. Slip florist's wire through the center. Pull the end of the wire through the circles. Glue the wire and wrap it with yellow crepe paper. This will keep it from sliding back. Cut four more circles slightly larger than the first ones. Slip them on the wire. Keep adding larger circles until the flower is the desired size. Make a calyx. Slip it on and glue it to the last petal. Wrap the wire with florist's tape. Turn the flower and stretch the tape as you go down the stem. To shape the flower, pull the petals out from the center.

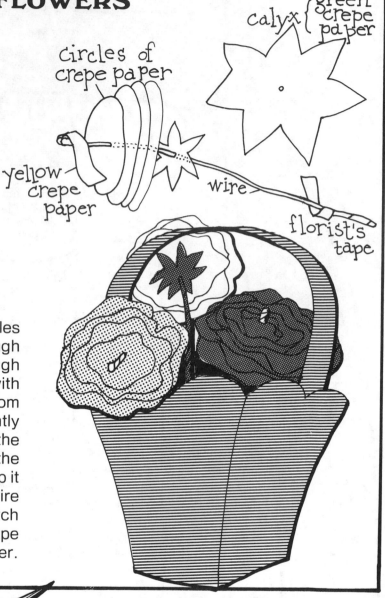

HIDING AMONG THE FLOWERS

''And when she could not longer hide him, she took for him an ark of bulrushes, and daubed it with slime and with pitch, and put the child therein; and she laid it in the flags by the river's brink.'' Exodus 2:3

Tell the story of Moses being hidden by his mother along the river bank. Bring some iris from home. Put a doll inside a small basket. Arrange the iris in a circle around the basket. Have the children retell the story using the props you provided.

MAKE A
MAY
BASKET

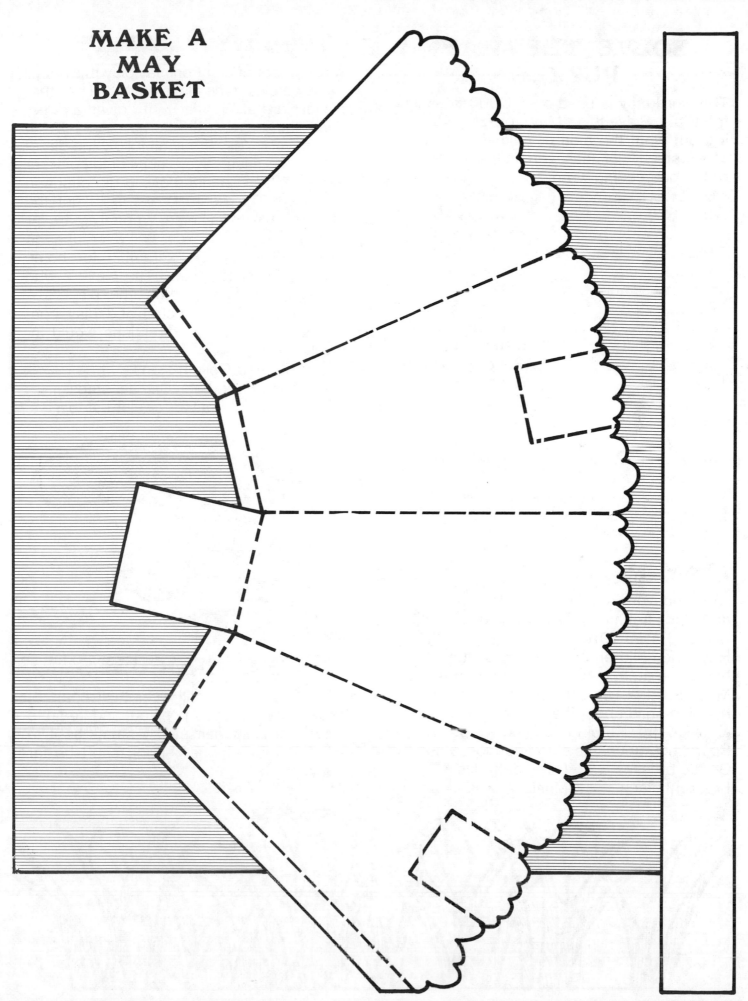

SOLVE THE MAY PUZZLE

The word *may* is used over 1,000 times in the Bible. Solve this ''May'' puzzle by finding out what the men or animals may do. The first letter of each word is the last letter of the preceeding word.

1. _ _ _   Genesis 1:20
2. _ _ _ _ _   Leviticus 19:25
3. _ _ _ _ _ _   Exodus 8:29
4. _ _ _ _ _   Exodus 35:34
5. _ _ _ _   Exodus 19:9
6. _ _ _ _   Exodus 23:12
7. _ _ _ _   Genesis 49:1
8. _ _ _ _ _ _   Exodus 5:9
9. _ _ _ _ _ _ _ _   Genesis 9:16
10. _ _ _ _ _   Genesis 11:4
11. _ _ _ _   Exodus 5:1
12. _ _ _   Exodus 21:14
13. _ _ _   Genesis 3:2
14. _ _ _ _   Genesis 24:49
15. _ _ _ _ _   Exodus 2:7

Answers: 1. fly, 2. yield, 3. depart, 4. teach, 5. hear, 6. rest, 7. tell, 8. labour, 9. remember, 10. reach, 11. hold, 12. die, 13. eat, 14. turn, 15. nurse

MAY IS . . .

''The heavens declare the glory of God; and the firmament showeth his handiwork.'' Psalm 19:1

Have the children observe the beauty God has given them in the lovely month of May. Make a list of two-word descriptions given by each child about the month of May. Encourage the use of interesting words.

Sparkling sunbeams   Bursting blossoms
Gentle breezes   Dewy daffodils
Fragrant lilacs   Musical birds

PLAY ''MAY I''

Any number of children may play this active game outside. One player is ''it.'' The other players are at ''home.'' ''It'' gives a direction. The players all chorus, ''May I?'' If ''it'' says, ''Yes,'' they all follow the direction. If ''it'' says, ''No,'' none of the players moves. ''It'' continues giving directions in this way. The goal of ''it'' is to get the players away from home. When they are far enough away, ''it'' calls, ''Everyone go home!'' The players scramble for home while ''it'' chases them. The players who are caught must help catch other players. A new ''it'' is then selected and play continues. Some sample directions would include:

Take 10 Goliath steps.
Take three baby Samuel steps.
Jog like Samson for eight steps.

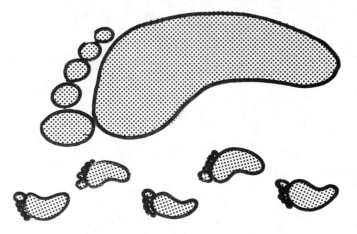

THE CROCUSES

While flower beds still wear their coats of snow, little crocuses peek out and begin to grow. They lift their sturdy stems as if to say, ''Winter's gone—spring can't be far away.''

Shining Star Publications, Copyright © 1985. A division of Good Apple, Inc.

HONOR MOTHERS
CELEBRATE MOTHER'S DAY

In 1907 Anna Jarvis of Grafton, Virginia, began a campaign to have a nationwide observance of Mother's Day. Her plan was to honor mothers on the second Sunday in May. She began the custom of people wearing carnations to show respect for their mothers. If a person's mother was living, that person would wear a red or pink carnation. If the mother was deceased, that person would wear a white carnation. President Woodrow Wilson signed a resolution which proclaimed Mother's Day as a national observance on May 9, 1914.

Make carnations to be worn on Mother's Day. For each flower cut fifteen 4-inch circles from pink or white tissue paper. Fold each circle into a pie-shaped wedge. Cut short snips around the outside edge. Unfold the circles. Begin placing them on a wire that has been knotted on the end. Add each of the circles to the wire. Fluff the flowers when all of them are on the wire. Wrap green florist's tape around the wire to form the stem.

On a Sunday in May

To celebrate Mother's Day

We put on a big display

TRIANGULAR TRIPLET

Write a triangular triplet to honor mothers. This is a three-lined poem which can be read starting from any point on the triangle.

BABIES IN THE CRADLE

Fold a handkerchief diagonally to form a triangle. Roll point B and point C to the center. Pull the underneath section of point A around to the back and up to the front. This will form a cradle for two sleeping babies inside.

Shining Star Publications, Copyright © 1985, A division of Good Apple, Inc.

OUR WONDERFUL MOTHERS

SAMUEL'S MOTHER

Prayed for him
Dedicated him to God
Visited once a year
Made a coat for him

Make a small apron. On the waistband write whose mother is being described. In the apron section, write some information that you know about this mother. A Biblical mother or your own mother may be used.

MOTHER WAS WORRIED

"The mother of Sisera looked out at a window, and cried through the lattice, Why is his chariot so long in coming? why tarry the wheels of his chariots?" Judges 5:28
Sisera's mother had reason to worry. Her son was an enemy of God's people. These enemies had been oppressing God's people for many years. God sent Deborah, a woman judge, to rescue His people. Sisera ran away from the battle, but he was killed in a most unusual way. Read about it in Judges 4:17-24.

MOTHER'S HELPER AWARD

_____

helped Mother by _____

_____

_____

on _____

_____
                    Signature

HONOR THY FATHER AND THY MOTHER

"Honour thy father and thy mother: that thy days may be long upon the land which the Lord thy God giveth thee." Exodus 20:12
Find the word *honor* in the dictionary. Select the meanings that fit this Scripture. Have the children list ways that they should honor their mothers and fathers.

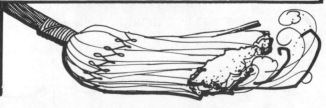

SET THE TABLE

If you were setting the table for a family and these people were the father and the child, who would the mother be?

1. Abraham	Isaac	_____
2. Jacob	Joseph	_____
3. Isaac	Esau	_____
4. Joseph	Jesus	_____

5. David	Solomon	_____
6. Zechariah	John the Baptist	_____
7. Elkanah	Samuel	_____
8. Boaz	Obed	_____

Answers:
1. Sarah, 2. Rachel, 3. Rebecca, 4. Mary, 5. Bath-sheba, 6. Elisabeth, 7. Hannah, 8. Ruth

MAKE A BANNER TO HONOR MOTHER

Supply a ¼'' dowel for each child. Have him fold a piece of construction paper over the dowel. Have each child write a message with a felt pen.

VALUES MOTHER TAUGHT ME

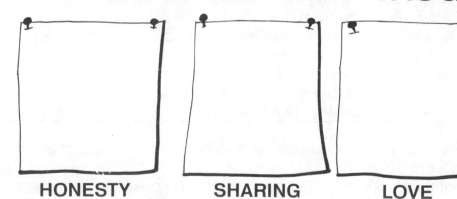

HONESTY   **SHARING**   **LOVE**   **PATIENCE**

"WHOSO KEEPETH THE LAW IS A WISE SON . . . ."

PROVERBS 28:7

Back the bulletin board with yellow paper. Discuss the values mothers have taught the children. Give them some magazines, and help them to make collages illustrating some of these values. Display the collages on the bulletin board.

MOTHER OF A SPECIAL CHILD

PUPPET CHARACTERS:

Narrator   Zechariah   Elisabeth   Gabriel   Mary   Neighbors

SCENE 1

In the temple

Narrator: Elisabeth and her husband, Zechariah, had been praying for a long time because they wanted to have a baby. They were getting old and had almost given up hope. But God answered their prayers in a very unusual way. While Zechariah was working in the temple one day, a stranger entered and frightened him.

Zechariah: (in fear) Who are you? What do you want?

Gabriel: Don't be frightened, Zechariah. I have good news for you. Your prayers have been heard. Your wife, Elisabeth, is going to have a son. You should name him John.

Zechariah: Can this be true? How do you know this?

Gabriel: God sent me as a messenger. He wanted me to tell you more about your son's birth. Many people will be happy when he is born. He will be great in the sight of the Lord. You must train him very carefully. He must not drink wine or any strong drink. He will be filled with the Holy Ghost the minute he is born.

Zechariah: If I had a son, I would do my best to train him and be a good father. But I cannot believe I will ever have a son.

Gabriel: Your son will be used to turn many people back to God. He will prepare the way for the coming of the Lord.

Zechariah: What you say seems so wonderful. But how can this be possible? Elisabeth and I are getting very old. We are past the years for having children.

Gabriel: I am Gabriel. I was sent to tell you these things. I am sorry that you cannot believe. Because of this unbelief, you will not be able to speak until the baby is born.

Narrator: The people who were praying in the temple wondered why Zechariah was inside so long. When he came out, they were puzzled because he could not speak. When he finished his work at the temple, he journeyed home. He wanted to tell Elisabeth all about it, but he could only write messages to tell her about his experience with the angel. The next few months were exciting. One day the family had a visit from Mary.

SCENE 2
In the home of Elisabeth

Mary: Elisabeth, it is so good to see you.

Elisabeth: It has been so long since we have seen you. I am so glad you came to visit.

Mary: I had to come. Angel Gabriel told me some exciting news about you. I just had to see if it is really true!

Elisabeth: It is true, Mary. After all these years of praying, God has heard our prayers. I am going to have a baby. It was so remarkable how God told us. About six months ago while Zechariah was working in the temple, Angel Gabriel appeared to him and said we would have a baby. Zechariah couldn't believe it could happen. Gabriel told him he would not be able to speak until the child is born.

Mary: It must be frustrating to be silent when he has so much to tell you!

Elisabeth: Oh, yes, it is hard sometimes, but it is so exciting to think that we are going to have a baby when we are so old.

Mary: There are many things to prepare for the baby. I will stay and help you.

Narrator: Mary stayed for three months. Then she returned home. The great day came quickly. Elisabeth had a beautiful baby boy. Her family and friends were very happy for her. On the eighth day, they circumcised him and called him Zechariah. This created a problem.

Elisabeth: No, we cannot name him Zechariah. His name is John.

Neighbors: No one in your family has that name. Why do you want to call him John? Let's ask Zechariah what he wants to name his son. Zechariah, what shall your son be called?

Zechariah: (Makes motions to indicate he wants to write. They bring him materials.) He writes: His name is John.

Narrator: Immediately after Zechariah named his son, he could speak. He began to praise God.

Zechariah: Blessed be the God of Israel for sending us this child, who will be called the prophet of God, to prepare the way for the Messiah.

Narrator: Elisabeth and Zechariah taught John all about God's love. Their son was very special. When he grew up, he was known as John the Baptist.

PENTECOST

Pentecost was first celebrated 50 days after the Passover Feast. Each year it is at the end of May or the beginning of June. Have the children count the days to see when it will be celebrated this year.

THE FEAST OF WEEKS

''Celebrate the Feast of Weeks with the firstfruits of the wheat harvest . . .'' Exodus 34:22 (NIV)

In the Old Testament, Pentecost was called the Feast of Weeks because it came 7 weeks after the Passover Feast. It is said that the Law was given to the Israelites 7 weeks after the first Passover. The Feast of Weeks was celebrated at the end of the harvest. The farmers were told not to glean in the corners of their fields so the poor people could find food. The Feast of Weeks provided a rest for everyone. No one was to work. They were to bring a wheat offering to the Lord. To follow the custom established by this festival, have the children bring food to share with the less fortunate.

SPEAKING IN OTHER TONGUES

''And they were all filled with the Holy Ghost, and began to speak with other tongues, as the Spirit gave them utterance.'' Acts 2:4

A very remarkable Pentecost occurred after the Passover when Jesus was crucified. The believers were all together in one place praying when suddenly there appeared cloven tongues like fire. They descended on the people. The people were filled with the Holy Spirit and began to speak in other languages. The disciples went out in the streets and preached to all of the people in their own languages. This amazed everyone. To help the children understand what a miracle this was teach them a few phrases in a foreign language. They will soon discover that it takes a lot of work to learn another language.

MEMORIAL DAY

TWO PRESIDENTS TO REMEMBER

On July 4, 1826, the country of America was 50 years old. John Adams, our second President, and Thomas Jefferson, our third President, were both very ill. Both of these men had helped to make our country free. John Adams had worked for independence, and Thomas Jefferson had written the Declaration of Independence. On this particular day, Thomas Jefferson was 83 years old and John Adams was 91. Both of the men died on the day they helped to create. Without their efforts there may not have been an Independence Day. Have the children find out more about these two Presidents.

CELEBRATE MEMORIAL DAY

The first Memorial Day occurred after the Civil War when the women of a small town in Mississippi decided to decorate the graves of not only their own soldiers, but also the graves of the Northern soldiers. This heartwarming gesture touched many lives. It helped to build a bridge of harmony between the North and the South. This day originally was to honor those who had died in the defense of our country. Now the day is set aside to honor all those who have lived before our time.

Have the children select a Biblical person whom they admire. Plan to honor this person on Memorial Day.

REMEMBER THE LIFE OF JESUS

"And he took bread, and gave thanks, and brake it, and gave unto them, saying, This is my body which is given for you: this do in remembrance of me." Luke 22:19

Jesus wanted His disciples to remember the purpose of His life and His death. This would be a good time to begin teaching the children about the Lord's Supper. Serve a sample communion explaining to the children the meaning of the bread and the wine (grape juice).

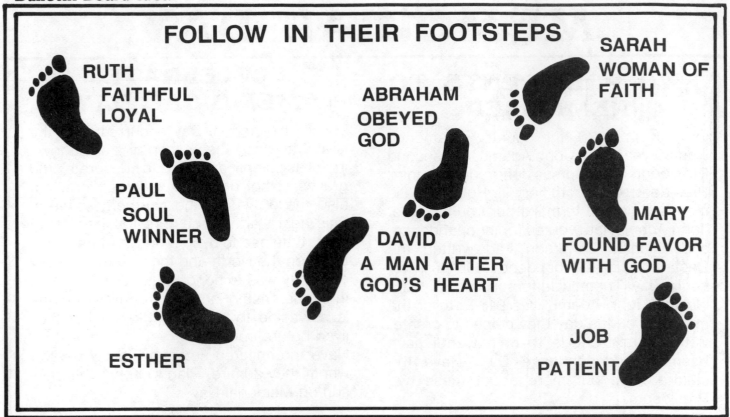

FOLLOW IN THEIR FOOTSTEPS

RUTH
FAITHFUL
LOYAL

ABRAHAM
OBEYED
GOD

SARAH
WOMAN OF
FAITH

PAUL
SOUL
WINNER

DAVID
A MAN AFTER
GOD'S HEART

MARY
FOUND FAVOR
WITH GOD

ESTHER

JOB
PATIENT

Back the bulletin board with blue butcher paper. Make black footsteps. Rather than using the people named above, the children may want to select their own favorite Bible people.

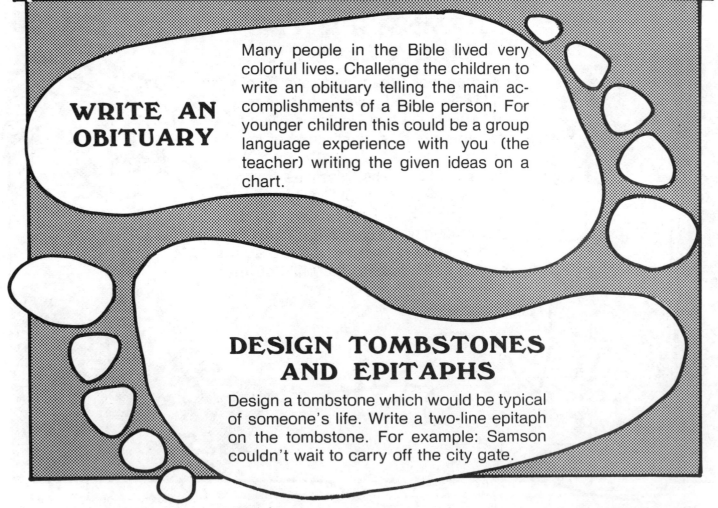

WRITE AN OBITUARY

Many people in the Bible lived very colorful lives. Challenge the children to write an obituary telling the main accomplishments of a Bible person. For younger children this could be a group language experience with you (the teacher) writing the given ideas on a chart.

DESIGN TOMBSTONES AND EPITAPHS

Design a tombstone which would be typical of someone's life. Write a two-line epitaph on the tombstone. For example: Samson couldn't wait to carry off the city gate.

Shining Star Publications, Copyright © 1985, A division of Good Apple, Inc.

JUNE

1 Plan to learn a new skill this summer.

2 Start a friendship chain.

5 Celebrate the last day of school.

6 Compose a Bible nursery rhyme.

7 Tell your mother your favorite Biblical child.

8 Find two bad children in the Bible.

9 List good children in the Bible.

10 Celebrate Children's Day.

11 Learn the Christian Flag Pledge.

12 Find out about Betsy Ross.

13 Memorize the Pledge to the Bible.

14 Celebrate Flag Day.

15 Learn about early U.S. flags.

16 Find roses for Father's Day.

17 Celebrate Father's Day.

18 Read about a Biblical father.

19 Ask your dad about his childhood.

20 Do a special favor for your dad.

21 Act out the story of the Prodigal Son with your friends.

22 Tell your father that you love him.

23 Make a bookmark for your father.

24 Find a father/son in the Bible that you didn't know about.

25 Plan a special surprise for your family.

26 Count the times you have obeyed your dad this week.

27 Look for animal shapes in the clouds.

28 Invite a friend over to play.

29 Learn a song about summer.

30 Learn Proverbs 3:1.

Shining Star Publications, Copyright © 1985, A division of Good Apple, Inc.

CELEBRATE THE LAST DAY OF SCHOOL

LAST DAY OF SCHOOL

When school gets out, I'm as happy as can be
For I don't have to work or study—my time is free.
I can jump, skate, swim and run
And have my friends over for a little fun.
We'll whip up a mountain of cookies to bake.
There will be jets, cars and airplanes to make.
Because summer is beckoning with its magnetic pull,
The best time of year is the last day of school.

START A FRIENDSHIP CHAIN

To help children keep in touch with their friends during the summer, start a friendship chain. Each child should be given a list of names and addresses of the children in the class. The first child on the list is given one link of a chain. He/She writes a short message on the link and mails it to the second person on the list. This person adds a link with a message and mails it on. At the end of the summer, the last child should return it to school so all of the messages can be shared.

RECIPE FOR A PERFECT SUMMER

If one plans goals during the summer, a feeling of accomplishment is achieved at summer's end. However, if one aimlessly goes through this prime time with no goals, time will just pass. Help the children to set realistic goals for the summer. This might include summer music programs, learning a new sport, participating in a service project for the community, or learning a new homemaking skill.

TRY THIS RECIPE FOR FUN

Melt together: 12 ounces of chocolate chips
10 ounces of almond bark
¼ cup of peanut butter
Stir together until it is well mixed.
Add 8 ounces of salted peanuts.
Drop in spoonfuls on waxed paper.
Allow to cool.

CELEBRATE FLAG DAY

"We will shout for joy when you are victorious and will lift up our banners in the name of our God. May the Lord grant all your requests." Psalm 20:5 (NIV)

★ THE STARS AND STRIPES

Many stories are told concerning the origin of our American flag. One story states that George Washington and his friends went to visit Betsy Ross with a drawing of a flag. It had red and white stripes with a field of blue for the white stars. Some people think that Betsy Ross made the first flag. The flag of the stars and stripes was adopted by Congress on June 14, 1777. Early flags were not all alike because no rules were made except that the flag should have thirteen stripes and thirteen stars to represent the thirteen colonies. A country's flag is important because the flag stands for the country's history and its hopes for the future. Have each child make a family flag that would represent values, history or people in the family. ★

BIBLICAL FLAGS

"Every man of the children of Israel shall pitch by his own standard, with the ensign of their father's house: far off about the tabernacle . . . ." Numbers 2:2

In early times banners were placed in conspicuous places so they could be easily seen. They were placed on poles or hilltops. They were used to call people to battle or to identify groups of people. When the Israelites were in the wilderness, they camped under their own banners.

Make flags representing the 12 tribes of Israel. ★

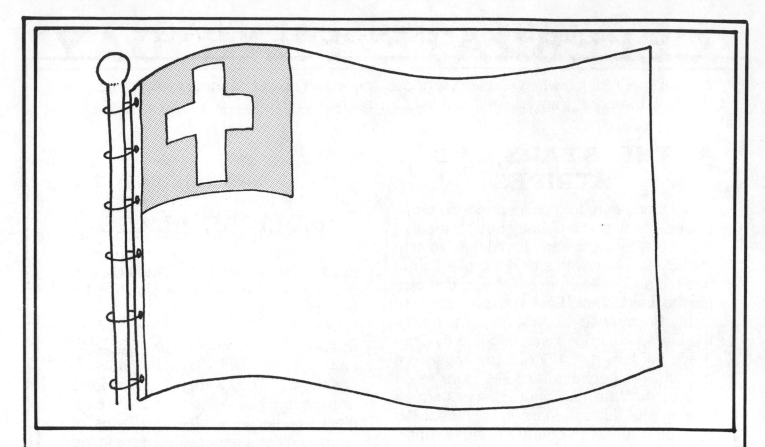

CHRISTIAN BANNERS

"He brought me to the banqueting house, and his banner over me was love."

Song of Solomon 2:4

BANNERS THEN AND NOW

In Biblical times it was a practice to give a defeated army a banner as a token of protection. It was regarded as the surest pledge of faithfulness. In Isaiah we read about God's banner.

"He will raise a banner for the nations and gather the exiles of Israel; he will assemble the scattered people of Judah from the four quarters of the earth." Isaiah 11:12 (NIV)

This is prophecy being fulfilled in our day. Discuss how these people who were scattered over the earth are returning to their homeland.

The idea for the Christian flag was conceived by Charles Overton in 1897 at his church in Coney Island, New York. The white portion of the flag represents purity and peace. The blue field symbolizes faith and trust. The red cross stands for the death of Christ when He shed His blood on the cross to save us from our sins.

Learn the pledge to the Christian flag:

I pledge allegiance to the Christian flag
And to the Savior for whose kingdom it stands;
One brotherhood uniting all mankind in service and love.

PLEDGE TO THE BIBLE

The Bible is God's banner of love which He provided for us. Teach the children the Pledge to the Bible.

I pledge allegiance to God's Holy Word.
I will make it a lamp unto my feet
And a light unto my path.
I will hide its words in my heart
That I might not sin against God.

A MOST UNUSUAL FLAG

"... Make thee a fiery serpent, and set it upon a pole: and it shall come to pass, that every one that is bitten, when he looketh upon it, shall live."
Numbers 21:8

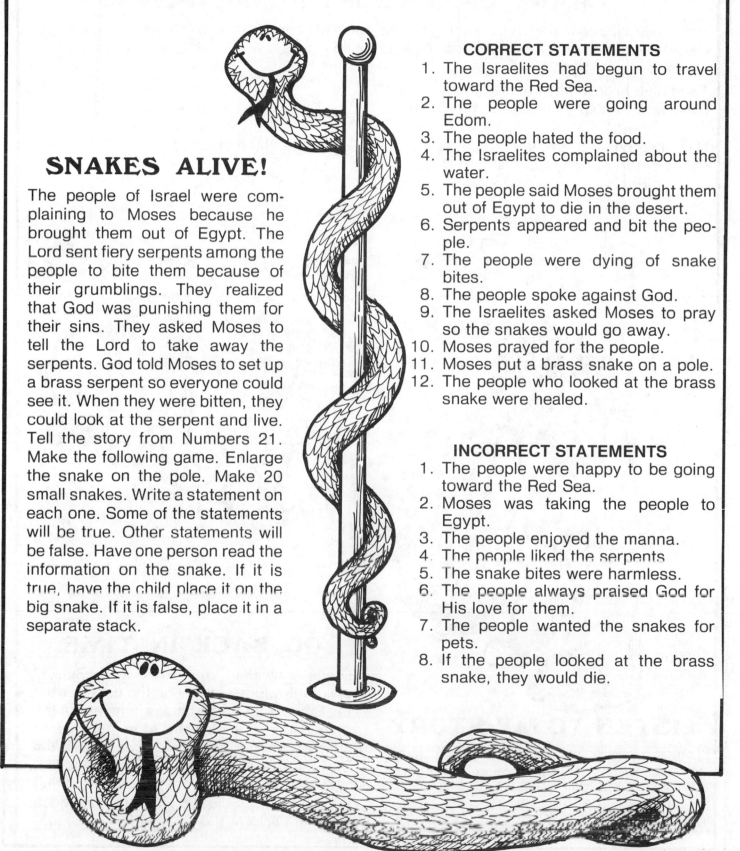

SNAKES ALIVE!

The people of Israel were complaining to Moses because he brought them out of Egypt. The Lord sent fiery serpents among the people to bite them because of their grumblings. They realized that God was punishing them for their sins. They asked Moses to tell the Lord to take away the serpents. God told Moses to set up a brass serpent so everyone could see it. When they were bitten, they could look at the serpent and live. Tell the story from Numbers 21. Make the following game. Enlarge the snake on the pole. Make 20 small snakes. Write a statement on each one. Some of the statements will be true. Other statements will be false. Have one person read the information on the snake. If it is true, have the child place it on the big snake. If it is false, place it in a separate stack.

CORRECT STATEMENTS

1. The Israelites had begun to travel toward the Red Sea.
2. The people were going around Edom.
3. The people hated the food.
4. The Israelites complained about the water.
5. The people said Moses brought them out of Egypt to die in the desert.
6. Serpents appeared and bit the people.
7. The people were dying of snake bites.
8. The people spoke against God.
9. The Israelites asked Moses to pray so the snakes would go away.
10. Moses prayed for the people.
11. Moses put a brass snake on a pole.
12. The people who looked at the brass snake were healed.

INCORRECT STATEMENTS

1. The people were happy to be going toward the Red Sea.
2. Moses was taking the people to Egypt.
3. The people enjoyed the manna.
4. The people liked the serpents.
5. The snake bites were harmless.
6. The people always praised God for His love for them.
7. The people wanted the snakes for pets.
8. If the people looked at the brass snake, they would die.

CELEBRATE CHILDREN'S DAY

MAKE UP A COUNTING RHYME

Have the children make up a counting rhyme. Have ten children stand in a line. As you say a line, one child should leave the line. As each child leaves, have something good that he is going to accomplish.

Ten little children all in a line
One went to help mother/then there were
    nine.
Nine little children swinging on a gate
One went to Sunday School/then there
    eight.

Eight little children . . .

Seven little children . . .

LISTEN TO MY STORY

Tell the story of a Biblical child using flannel-backed figures. Leave the figures for the children to retell the story to one another. This is a good review. In addition it helps develop good listening skills.

GO BACK IN TIME

Dress a child in your room as a Biblical child. Introduce him/her as the person from the Bible. Give a little background about the person and then tell the story. The other children should be encouraged to ask the Biblical child questions about his/her life. Younger children may need help answering the questions. Select a different child each week to perform this special function.

BIBLICAL CHILDREN

"Even a child is known by his doings, whether his work be pure, and whether it be right."
Proverbs 20:11

MAKE A MURAL OF BIBLICAL CHILDREN

Have the students select children from the Bible. Instruct the students to lie on butcher paper and trace around their bodies individually. Have the students draw in features and Biblical clothing. Display these Bible children on a long wall in the hall. The older children should be encouraged to find out as much as possible about their Bible children.

GOOD CHILDREN

Isaac	Genesis 22:6-10
Joseph	Genesis 45:9-10
Jephthah's child	Judges 11:3-40
Samuel	I Samuel 2
David	I Samuel 17
Josiah	II Chronicles 34
Esther	Esther 2:20
Daniel	Daniel 1
John the Baptist	Luke 1:57-80
Jesus	Luke 2:41-52
Timothy	II Timothy 3:15
Moses	Exodus 2

BAD CHILDREN

The Bible tells us about bad children as well as good children. Find out what these children did that displeased God and their parents.

Esau	Genesis 26:34-35
Eli's sons	I Samuel 2:12-17
Samuel's sons	I Samuel 8:3
Absalom	II Samuel 15:10
Adonijah	I Kings 1:5-6
Children who made fun of Elisha	II Kings 2:23

WRITE BIBLICAL NURSERY RHYMES

To help the children remember some of the Biblical characters and what they did, write some nursery rhymes.

SONS OF JACOB

The sons of Jacob went over the hill
To fetch some food and fodder.
Joseph was found, and Jacob moved down
To Egypt with his sons and daughter.

NEHEMIAH, NEHEMIAH

Nehemiah, Nehemiah got on the ball.
Nehemiah, Nehemiah built up the wall.
All the evil forces and all the evil men
Couldn't keep Nehemiah from building the wall again.

The following are nursery rhyme ideas:
1. Moses in the bulrushes.
2. Shadrach, Meshach and Abed-nego in the fiery furnace.
3. Samuel with Eli, the priest.
4. David, a shepherd who became king.
5. Isaac, father of Jacob and Esau.
6. Esther, a queen who saved the Jews.
7. Daniel in the lion's den.
8. John the Baptist, a young preacher.

LEARN A NEW PROVERB

Each week post a proverb that relates to children. Discuss it. Each day say the proverb. At the end of the week, the children should know it well.

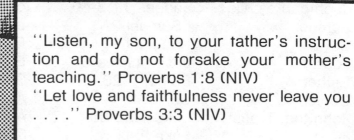

"Listen, my son, to your father's instruction and do not forsake your mother's teaching." Proverbs 1:8 (NIV)
"Let love and faithfulness never leave you . . . ." Proverbs 3:3 (NIV)

WARM FUZZIES

by Joe Wayman

1. A soft warm fuzzy is a very special thing, It comes in many sizes, shapes and colors. No matter how or why or where, when ever they are given, warm fuzzies make a sad heart sing. Make someone sing. Just show them you care. Give a soft warm fuzzy away. They're easy to share.

2. Everyone who's listening to this simple song,
Has a treasure trove of fuzzies waiting to belong
In someone else's pocket or sitting on their heart,
Give a fuzzy away, hear a new song start.

3. Give a fuzzy to a stranger and a smile will come your way,
Give a fuzzy to a friend if he is sad.
Give a fuzzy everytime you see that someone else is hurting,
Fuzzies help another know you understand.

4. For every fuzzy given, you will find that in return,
Two or more will always seem to come your way.
But keep them to yourself and hidden in a private place,
And even those you have will die and fade away.

CELEBRATE FATHER'S DAY

GOD—OUR HEAVENLY FATHER

WANTS TO SEE OUR LIGHT SHINE

SENT HIS SON TO DIE FOR US

GIVES US GOOD GIFTS

CREATED THE WORLD

WILL TEACH US WHAT TO SAY

PROVIDES FOR US

IS PREPARING A MANSION FOR US

WANTS US TO WORSHIP HIM ONLY

CELEBRATE FATHER'S DAY

Father's Day is celebrated on the third Sunday in June. Mrs. John Bruce Dodd is given credit for promoting the day. After hearing a Mother's Day sermon, she decided that a day should also be set aside for fathers. The purpose for the day was to build closer home relations and to encourage Biblical standards in developing father-child rapport. A red rose is to be worn on the day to honor a father who is living. A white rose is to be worn to honor a father who is deceased.

WISE CHILD AWARD

"A wise son maketh a glad father . . . ."

Proverbs 10:1

_____

made a wise decision in obeying his/her heavenly Father by

_____

The child was also wise when he/she obeyed his/her earthly father by

_____

FATHER-SON

"The father of the righteous shall greatly rejoice: and he that begetteth a wise child shall have joy of him."

Proverbs 23:24

THIS IS MY SON

Plan an ongoing project. Supply large and small neckties made of colorful construction paper. See how many father-son combinations the children can provide from the Bible. They must be able to supply one Biblical fact about either the father or the son. The name of the father can only be used once. The other sons can be listed beside his tie. Display the sons' neckties beside the father's tie. Group the neckties by families, and display around the room. Encourage the fathers of the children to assist in this project.

FACT:
   Jonathan was one of David's best friends.

THE PRODIGAL SON

Jesus told us a parable about a father and his son in Luke 15:11-32. Tell the story of the prodigal son. Have your children give the play by that name from *Acting for God* by Kathy Jones. This is a Shining Star Publication.

INTERVIEW FATHERS

Ask the children to interview their fathers. Give a list of questions to ask. These might include:
   What was the most important thing your father taught you?
   What did you like best about your father?
   Tell me about a kind deed you did when you were little.
   How did you learn about God?
   What was the happiest time of your childhood?
   What is the most important idea you want to teach me?

Shining Star Publications, Copyright © 1985, A division of Good Apple, Inc.

WHO IS THIS FATHER?

Make descriptive word sketches of fathers in the Bible. Have the children guess whom you are describing. Examples might include:

I was the first man on Earth.
I had a son who became a murderer.
My wife was Eve.

I had twelve sons. One of them was sold by his brothers. I sent some of my sons to Egypt to buy food. I loved my son, Benjamin, very much. I went to Egypt to live when I was old.

One of my sons was crowned king over Israel while Saul was still king. He did not become king right away. Instead, he went back to take care of my sheep.

The older children may want to make up descriptions of their own. Some fathers could be: Gideon, Abraham, Isaac, Esau, Zebedee, David, Solomon, Elkanah, Boaz, or Ahab.

A FATHER IS . . .

For younger children make a chart with the above caption. Have them give their ideas about what a father is to them. Write these ideas on the chart. The older children could be given an individual assignment to write the things they think a father is to them. You could then make a composite of the ideas. This would make a good take-home paper. Fathers would enjoy seeing themselves through the eyes of their children.

MAKE A BOOKMARK FOR DAD

Give each child a piece of colorful poster board. Have him think of a saying which would be appropriate for his father. Cover the bookmark with clear Con-Tact to preserve it.

JULY

1 Learn about Ehud.

2 Play a Bible game.

3 Plan a picnic.

4 Celebrate Independence Day.

5 List your freedoms.

6 Thank God for freedom.

7 Pray for people not free.

8 Ask about a Bible Freedom Fighter.

9 Learn about the Liberty Bell.

10 Memorize Leviticus 25:10.

11 Read about Onesimus.

12 Find out about U.S. slaves.

13 How many disciples were fishermen?

14 Ask your dad to take you fishing.

15 Learn how to be a fisher of men.

16 Learn to tie some knots.

17 Make a fishnet.

18 Read about Jonah.

19 Pantomime Jonah with a friend.

20 Plan an ideal vacation.

21 Learn about Biblical travel.

22

23 Estimate the distance to your vacation spot.

24 Make a map of Israel.

25 Find 2 cities in Israel.

26 Locate a river in Israel.

27

28 Name six Bible people who took trips.

29 Learn John 8:32.

30 Learn about Deborah.

31 Draw a map of your neighborhood.

Shining Star Publications, Copyright © 1985, A division of Good Apple, Inc.

CELEBRATE INDEPENDENCE DAY

THEY FOUGHT FOR FREEDOM

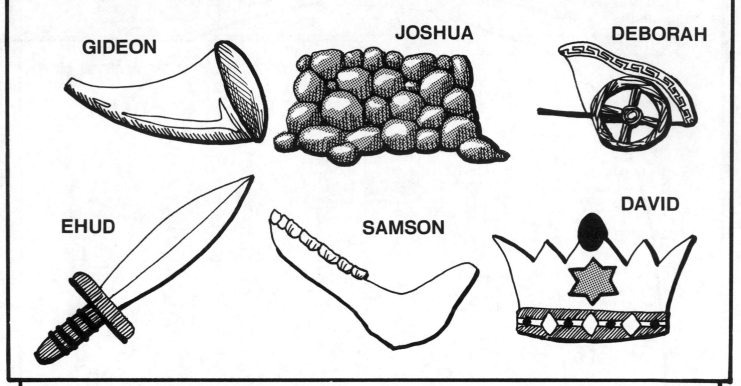

Cover the bulletin board with blue butcher paper. Enlarge the pictures. Cover the sword with aluminum foil. Tell the stories of how each of the people fought for freedom.

GIDEON

Gideon's fight against the Midianites is recorded in Judges 6-7.

JOSHUA

The entire book of Joshua tells how this freedom fighter led his people to victory in conquering the Promised Land.

DEBORAH

Deborah defeated the Canaanites. Read about her in Judges 4-5.

SAMSON

This strong man fought the Philistines who were constantly at war with his country. His story is told in Judges 13-16.

EHUD

Ehud's fight was against the Moabites. His story of intrigue is told in Judges 3:12-30.

DAVID

King David expanded the country's boundaries by defeating many enemies. II Samuel records his adventures.

Games for Gideon, Joshua, Deborah, Samson and David can be found in the book *Breaking into Bible Games*. This is a Shining Star Publication.

SYMBOL OF AMERICAN FREEDOM

★★★★★★★★★★★★★★★★★★★★★★★★★★★★★★★★

THE LIBERTY BELL

In the early days of our country, the Liberty Bell was used to call the people of Philadelphia together for important announcements. On July 8, 1776, the people assembled to hear the Declaration of Independence read. The country had been ruled by England. Now it would rule itself. The bell rang for the last time on July 8, 1935. While the bell was ringing on that day, a huge crack tore across it. Even though it is silent, the bell still symbolizes freedom. Have the children learn the Bible verse written on the bell (Leviticus 25:10).

SILVER TRUMPETS

''Make two trumpets of hammered silver, and use them for calling the community together and for having the camps set out.'' Numbers 10:2 (NIV) Just as the Liberty Bell was used to call the people of Philadelphia, so the silver trumpets were used to call the people of Israel. When both trumpets sounded, the whole community was to assemble. If only one trumpet sounded, the leaders were to assemble. They were also to blow their trumpets when they broke camp to move on to another place. Trumpets were blown to announce the feasts. Make silver trumpets from aluminum foil.

★★★★★★★★★★★★★★★

LET FREEDOM RING

_____

has learned the Bible verse imprinted on the Liberty Bell. ''. . . proclaim liberty throughout all of the land unto all the inhabitants thereof. . . .''
Leviticus 25:10

_____
Signature

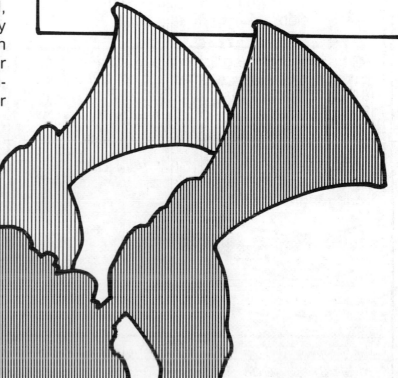

THE SHIELD OF THE UNITED STATES

The shield of the United States uses the stars and stripes from the American flag on the background. In the foreground is the national bird, the eagle. A shield is a defensive piece of armor to protect the body in battle. The Bible tells us to put on the whole armor of God including the shield of faith so that we can reject evil forces. Read Ephesians 6:10-18. Have the children design a Biblical shield.

THE STATUE OF LIBERTY

The Statue of Liberty stands majestically in the New York harbor. A token of friendship from the people of France, it has symbolized hope for many immigrants who had been downtrodden. When ships carrying immigrants enter the harbor, the magnificent statue seems to help them banish thoughts of the past to make way for future hopes. The Bible is also a very real source of hope. Jesus says, ''Come to me, all you who are weary and burdened, and I will give you rest.'' Matthew 11:28 (NIV) Read Matthew 11:28-30. Have the children write letters as though they were Jesus inviting all who have problems to come to Him.

OUR COUNTRY'S BIRTHDAY

Long ago some men assembled with Thomas Jefferson to write a document called ''The Declaration of Independence.'' The people said in this document that they wanted to be an independent country that could make its own laws and rule itself. This paper was signed on July 4, 1776. This date is called our country's birthday. Make a red, white and blue birthday cake to celebrate the occasion.

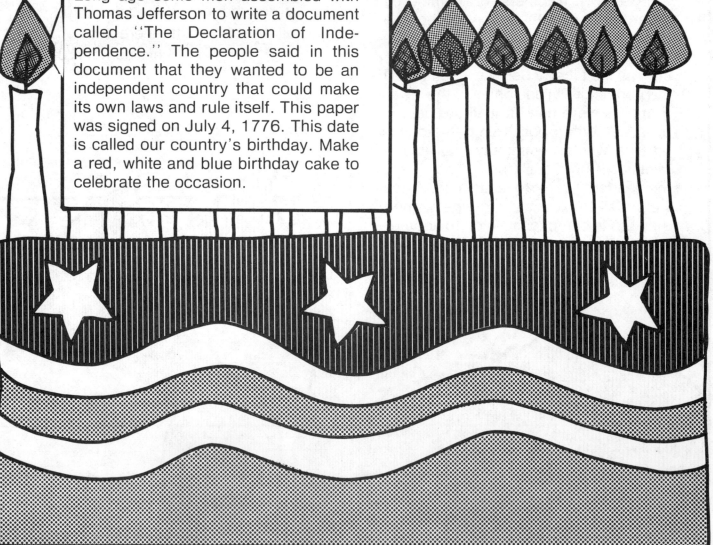

SIGNERS OF THE DECLARATION OF INDEPENDENCE

After the Declaration of Independence was written, men had to be very brave to sign it. Doing so would mean an about-face from the direction in which they were going. They would be considered traitors to their mother country. John Hancock was the first person to sign the Declaration of Independence. He wrote in very large script so everyone would know how strongly he felt about his decision.

When the disciples of Jesus started to follow Him, the decision they made was even more drastic. It would change the course of the whole world. Find the disciples' names in the Word Search below. Their names will all be found vertically or horizontally.

1. Andrew, 2. Bartholomew, 3. James, 4. James, 5. John, 6. Judas, 7. Jude, 8. Matthew, 9. Peter, 10. Philip, 11. Simon, 12. Thomas

J	A	M	E	S	J	T	L	A	C	E
B	A	R	T	H	O	L	O	M	E	W
P	N	D	E	T	H	O	M	A	S	M
H	D	F	I	J	N	H	B	T	L	N
I	R	K	G	U	M	P	E	T	E	R
L	E	J	U	D	E	O	P	H	Q	R
I	W	T	J	A	M	E	S	E	S	U
P	A	D	I	S	O	N	X	W	V	A
Q	P	T	L	V	S	I	M	O	N	P

A MOST UNUSUAL PARADE

When the Israelites were told to capture the city of Jericho, the battle plan included a parade around the city for seven days. Read about this parade in Joshua 6:1-27. Play the game entitled "Walk Around Jericho" from *Breaking into Bible Games*, pages 23-27. This is a Shining Star Publication.

EVERYBODY LOVES A PARADE

The Fourth of July brings many parades of celebration. Make drums to use in your parade.

Cover a coffee can with red, white and blue paper. Glue thin strips of black paper diagonally around the can. Attach narrow pieces of black paper to the top and bottom of the can. Cut ¼'' dowels to make drum sticks.

NOT EVERYONE ENJOYED FREEDOM

The book of Philemon tells the story of a slave who had run away and had been converted through the ministry of Paul. Paul was sending the slave back to Philemon. This was a very dangerous move since runaway slaves were treated very cruelly when they were found. They were often branded on the forehead. Sometimes they were crucified as an example to other slaves who were thinking of trying to escape from their masters. Paul wrote this letter to Philemon and give it to Onesimus to give to his master. The letter asks Philemon to accept Onesimus as a brother and to treat him kindly. Have the children role play what they think could have happened when Onesimus returned to his master.

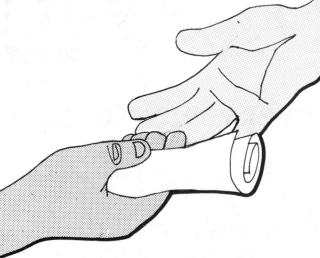

ABOLISHING SLAVERY IN THE UNITED STATES

When President Lincoln told the country that he believed the South should not leave the nation, he used a Scripture quotation to state his position. Matthew 12:25 states: ''. . . Every kingdom divided against itself is brought to desolation; and every city or house divided against itself shall not stand.'' Negro slavery was the issue that divided the country. It was abolished after the war.

GOD LOVES SLAVES, TOO

Hagar was the slave of Sarah, Abraham's wife. Sometimes Sarah was not kind to her slave. Once she mistreated her so badly that she ran away into the desert. An angel of the Lord came to her and told her to go back to Sarah. He also told her that she was going to have a baby and a nation would be produced from this child. Tell the story from Genesis 16. Have the children do a television interview to find out how Hagar felt when she was mistreated, when she went into the desert, and when an angel spoke to her. Ask her also how she knew that God loved her even though she was a slave.

FREEDOM VERSES TO LEARN

John 8:32
John 8:36
Galations 5:1
Galations 3:28

GONE FISHING

I WILL MAKE YOU FISHERS OF MEN

". . . they straightway left their nets, and followed him.'' (Matthew 4:20) Some of the disciples of Jesus were fishermen. One day as Jesus was walking by the Sea of Galilee, He called Simon and Andrew to be His followers. Later He saw James and John in the fishing boat with their father, Zebedee, mending their nets. He called them, and immediately they left their father to follow Jesus. Special knots were necessary to mend the nets. Teach the children some simple knots.

MIRACLE OF THE FISHES

". . . Launch out into the deep, and let down your nets for a draught.'' Luke 5:4 After Jesus had used one of the fishing boats as a platform from which to speak to the people, He told the disciples to go out into the sea and let down their nets. Simon told Him that they had fished all night and had caught nothing. But at His word, they decided to go out to fish. When they let down the nets, so many fish were caught that the nets began to break. They called for help. Both of the boats were filled so full that they began to sink. What a miracle!

Make fish nets from crepe paper. Keeping it folded cut narrow strips almost to the fold. Turn the paper to the other side and cut between the first cuttings again cutting almost to the fold. Do not cut through the fold. Carefully open the crepe paper. Suspend it from the ceiling. Have the children make different kinds of fish. Glue or staple these to the net.

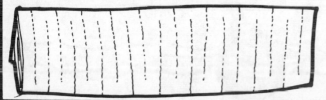

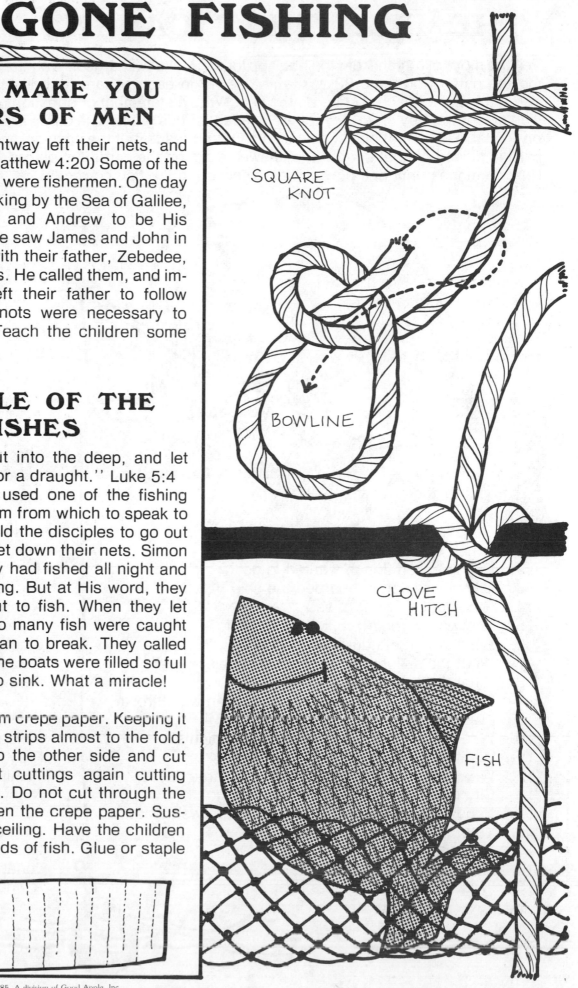

SQUARE KNOT

BOWLINE

CLOVE HITCH

FISH

THE FISH THAT CAUGHT A MAN

Tell the story of Jonah from the book of Jonah. Make two large fish on gray poster board using the pattern on page 83. Write an answer in each square on both fish. Make 18 little cards the size of each square on the fish. Write a statement or question on each card. Provide an answer key. Two players are needed for this game. The cards are placed face down on the table. The first player selects a card and reads it. If the answer is on his/her fish, the card is placed on that spot. If the answer is not on the card, it is placed back on the table. Play continues until one player wins by covering the fish correctly.

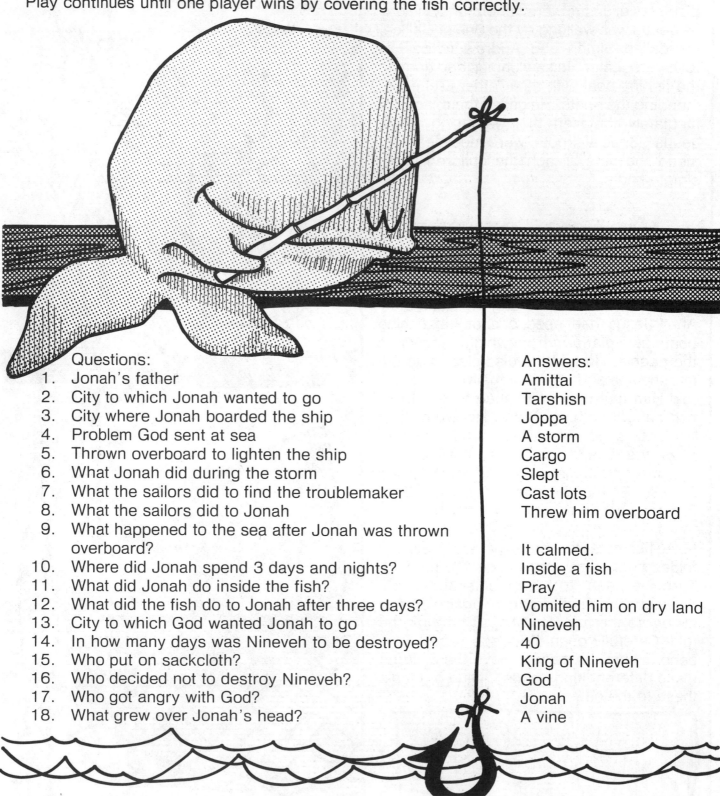

Questions:

1. Jonah's father
2. City to which Jonah wanted to go
3. City where Jonah boarded the ship
4. Problem God sent at sea
5. Thrown overboard to lighten the ship
6. What Jonah did during the storm
7. What the sailors did to find the troublemaker
8. What the sailors did to Jonah
9. What happened to the sea after Jonah was thrown overboard?
10. Where did Jonah spend 3 days and nights?
11. What did Jonah do inside the fish?
12. What did the fish do to Jonah after three days?
13. City to which God wanted Jonah to go
14. In how many days was Nineveh to be destroyed?
15. Who put on sackcloth?
16. Who decided not to destroy Nineveh?
17. Who got angry with God?
18. What grew over Jonah's head?

Answers:

Amittai
Tarshish
Joppa
A storm
Cargo
Slept
Cast lots
Threw him overboard

It calmed.
Inside a fish
Pray
Vomited him on dry land
Nineveh
40
King of Nineveh
God
Jonah
A vine

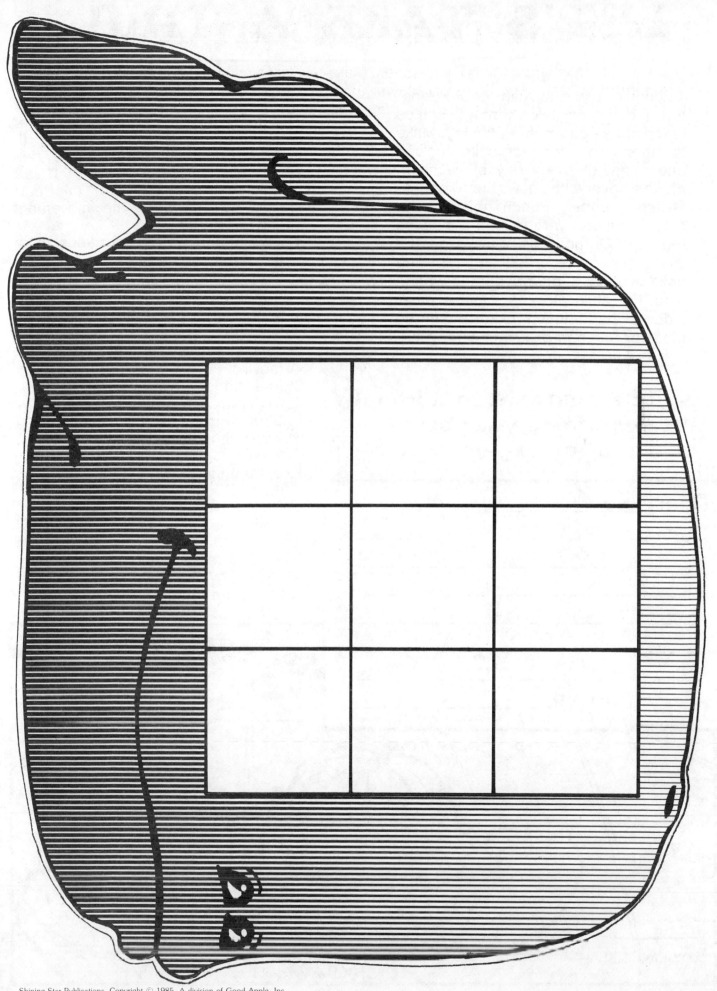

LET'S TAKE A TRIP

A FINGER GAME FOR TRAVELING

Taking a vacation can be exciting. Reliving the occasion through stories and pictures can multiply the joy. Make vacation books for each child. Include one page for every day of vacation. Make a cover with poster board or construction paper. Punch holes in the side and insert yarn to hold the pages together. On one side of the page, the event can be recorded either by the child writing it or the parent writing what the child dictates. On the other side, a hand-drawn picture can be made or photographs can be mounted.

This game starts with just the finger and thumb moving back and forth touching one another. Each verse adds another part of the body. As each part is added, movement with this part should be added to the movement already in progress.

1. One finger, one thumb; keep them moving.
   One finger, one thumb; keep them moving.
   One finger, one thumb; keep them moving.
2. Two fingers, two thumbs; keep them moving . . . .
3. Four fingers, two thumbs . . . .
4. Six fingers, two thumbs . . . .
5. Eight fingers, two thumbs . . . .
6. Eight fingers, two thumbs, one hand . . . .
7. Eight fingers, two thumbs, two hands . . . .

On successive verses add arms, feet, legs and head until finally the sequence is:

Eight fingers, two thumbs, two hands, two arms, two feet, two legs, one head; keep them moving.

Write a postcard to a friend describing your best vacation experience.

Dear_____,
_____
_____
_____
_____
_____
         From, _____

Shining Star Publications. Copyright © 1985. A division of Good Apple. Inc.

LEARN ABOUT THE COUNTRY OF ISRAEL

NORTH, SOUTH, EAST, WEST

To learn directions in Israel, give each child a map of the country. Divide it into 4 sections with thin strips of construction paper. Give each child 4 letters: N, S, E, W. Have him place the letters in the proper places on the country. You might then give various directions to help the children identify sections of the country. For example, "Put your finger on the city in the northern section that is at the top of the Sea of Galilee. Put your thumb on the sea in the southern section of the map."

BE A TOUR GUIDE IN ISRAEL

Give each child a different city in Israel. Enlist the help of the parents to assist their child in finding out at least one reason why this city was mentioned in the Bible. At the next class session, start a tour through Israel by stopping at each city long enough for the "Tour Guide" to give the information he/she has found.

MAKE A RELIEF MAP

To learn about the mountains and lowlands in the country of Israel, have the children make a salt and flour relief map. To make the dough, mix 1 part salt, 2 parts flour and one part water. Knead the dough until it holds together well. Have them show heights on the map by building up the dough. Allow it to dry. Paint the mountains brown and the lowlands green.

MAKE A PUZZLE

Draw a map of Israel. Write in the names of important cities. Mount it on poster board. Cut it apart. Have the children reassemble it. In doing so, they will learn the sections where the cities are located.

TRAVEL LONG AGO

WAYS TO TRAVEL

Traveling was often done simply by walking. Sometimes the traveler rode a camel, donkey, horse, or a mule. Robbers attacked frequently so people grouped together for safety when possible. A hard day's journey would be about 25 miles. If the group was large, it would progress only 10 miles in a day. The distance from one place to another was stated in time required to get to that place. For example, it was a three day's journey to visit my friend. Compare a day's journey of modern times with long ago—in a car, in a bus, in an airplane, in a rocket. Calculate how long it would take to get to a favorite vacation spot if the traveler had to walk at the rate of 25 miles a day.

OVERNIGHT LODGING

The traveler in the Old Testament would find no fancy motels. Instead, only a place of shelter would be found. However, people considered hospitality a religious duty, so people often offered travelers their guest room if one was available. This little room was usually located on the roof of the house. Travelers were required to take food not only for themselves, but also for any animals they would have with them on the trip. Any supplies for personal grooming would have to be brought from home. Ask the children to pack an imaginary bag to include all the things a traveler would have to carry on a trip long ago.

GROUP ACTIVITY ON TRAVELING

Think of Bible people who went on trips. Start the activity by saying, ''I went on a trip, and I took _____ with me.'' The one who guesses the correct answer gets to be ''It.''
Examples:

I went on a trip, and I took gold, frankincense and
myrrh with me.   Wise men

I went on a trip, and I took a knife, some wood, and
my son with me.   Abraham

I went on a trip, and I took my little son and my wife
with me. We were in a hurry to escape.   Joseph,
                                                                                          father of
                                                                                          Jesus

AUGUST

1 Read about Naomi's family. Ruth 1	**2** Be thoughtful to your family.	**3** Tell about past family fun.	**4** Pray for your family.	**5** Learn Psalm 122:1.	**6** Plan a camping trip.	**7** Find out about camping in the Bible.
8 Draw a Biblical tent.	**9** Tell why you would like to live in a tent.	**10** Go swimming.	**11** Read about the bonfire in Ephesus. Acts 19	**12** Go skating with your family.	**13** Create a holiday for August.	**14** Memorize Psalm 125:2.
15 Think about your good qualities.	**16** Ask your mother what she likes best about you.	**17** Tell your mother what you like best about her.	**18** Take a walk in the woods.	**19** Visit a friend.	**20** Learn Proverbs 12:1a.	**21** Write a letter to a friend.
22 Thank God for your home.	**23** Plan one way to improve in school.	**24** Go for a bike ride.	**25** Plan a picnic with your friends.	**26** Learn Psalm 24:1, 2	**27** Water the flowers.	**28** Read the newspaper.
29 Pray for your church.	**30** Learn Proverbs 15:2.	**31** Draw a cartoon.				

CELEBRATE A WONDERFUL FAMILY

THE FAMILY PORTRAIT

Instruct the children to draw a family portrait. Under each member's picture, write the best attribute of that person.

Peaches (faithful)   Sue (plays fairly)   David (good sport)   Mother (loving)   Father (kind)   Floof (very soft)

PLAY FAMILY TIC-TAC-TOE

Place nine chairs in the front of the room. Divide the children into 2 teams. Give one team a set of X's. Give the other team a set of O's. Select children to pantomime activities you have written on slips of paper. The first team to guess the family or event correctly may place one of their team members in a chair. The next participant then pantomimes. The first team to get three people in a row in the chairs is the winner.

SUGGESTED FAMILY EVENTS

1. Miriam putting Moses in the water.
2. Hannah putting coat on Samuel.
3. Moses and Aaron talking to Pharaoh.
4. Wise men bringing gifts to Jesus.
5. Zechariah telling Elisabeth about the angel's visit.
6. Joseph's brothers plotting to get rid of him.
7. Joseph telling his father about his dreams.
8. Daniel being put in the lion's den.
9. Moses parting the Red Sea or discovering a burning bush.

FAMILY WORD PLAY

Read the story to the children. As the different persons are named, the action given should be performed.

Jacob—Lift hand over head and say, "He's the father."
Joseph—Wrap arms around self as if to hug.
    Say, "He's the father's favorite son."
Brothers—Make a mean expression on the face. Place hands on hips. Say, "They're the jealous ones."

JACOB AND HIS SONS

Long, long ago there lived a man named Jacob (   ) who had 12 sons. They all lived together in the land of Canaan. Now Jacob (   ) loved Joseph (   ) more than all the other brothers (   ). Jacob (   ) had a special coat of many colors made for Joseph (   ). When the brothers (   ) saw that Jacob (   ) loved Joseph (   ) more than all the other brothers (   ), they hated Joseph (   ) and would not speak pleasantly to Joseph (   ).

One night Joseph (   ) had a dream. Joseph (   ) told his brothers (   ) the dream. The brothers (   ) hated Joseph (   ) all the more. In the dream Joseph (   ) said the brothers (   ) were binding sheaves of wheat in the field when Joseph's (   ) sheaf arose and the sheaves of the brothers (   ) bowed down to Joseph (   ).

Joseph (   ) had another dream which he told his brothers (   ). In this dream the sun, moon, and stars all bowed down to Joseph (   ). Joseph (   ) told his dream to Jacob (   ). Jacob (   ) scolded Joseph (   ). His brothers (   ) were angry.

One day the brothers (   ) went to feed Jacob's (   ) sheep in Shechem. Jacob (   ) sent Joseph (   ) to check on his brothers (   ). When the brothers (   ) saw Joseph (   ) coming, they decided to try to kill Joseph (   ). The brothers (   ) cast Joseph (   ) into a pit. Later some men came by. The brothers (   ) decided to sell Joseph (   ) for 20 pieces of silver. The brothers (   ) dipped Joseph's (   ) coat into some animal blood. The brothers (   ) took the coat to Jacob (   ). They told Jacob (   ) that they had found the coat. Jacob (   ) thought some wild animal had killed Joseph (   ). How sad Jacob (   ) was. Jacob (   ) mourned many days for his son Joseph (   ).

This story may be continued from Genesis 37 as far as you want to pursue it.

FAMILY FUN

FUNNY FACES

Make open-faced sandwiches for each member of the family. Spread a slice of bread with a thin layer of deviled ham. Make a face on the bread. Use carrot curls or coconut for hair, sliced olives for the eyes, pimento for the mouth, carrot or celery wedge for the nose, sliced radishes for the cheeks, and pepper slices for the eyebrows.

COME TO OUR PARTY

Date _____

Time _____

Cost _____

Place _____

FAMILY SKATE NIGHT

Plan a skating party for the whole family. Instruct the children on how to write invitations including the date, time, place, and cost for the event. Design awards for individual accomplishments. For little ones who have never been on skates before, a certificate for making it around the rink could be awarded. Older children's awards should be based on their abilities.

SKATING AWARD

This is to certify that

_____

was a good skater on _____

because _____

_____

Signature

Shining Star Publications, Copyright © 1985, A division of Good Apple, Inc.

THERE IS NO OTHER

Verse 3. There is no other like my brother;
He's a friend to me.
There is no other like my brother;
We are family.

Verse 4. There is no other like my sister;
She helps me each day.
There is no other like my sister;
I think she's okay.

**Words and Music
by
Kathy Jones**

CREATE A HOLIDAY

START A TRADITION

The month of August has no official holidays. Brainstorm to try to find a holiday the children would like to create. Help develop ways to celebrate the day. What foods will be eaten? What practices will be followed? What goals will be accomplished? One sample holiday might be Friendship Day. One goal could be to develop a new friendship by taking a basket of goodies to the house of an acquaintance. After enjoying the contents of the basket together, the person should be encouraged to refill the basket and take it to another person's house during the month of August.

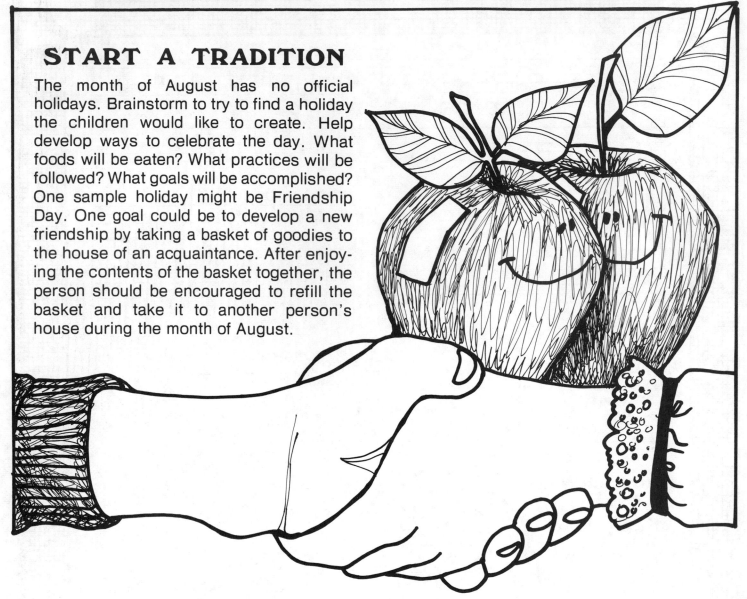

FRIENDSHIP PROVERBS

Learn or make up proverbs about friends.
"A friend loveth at all times . . . ."
Proverbs 17:17
"A man that hath friends must show himself friendly: and there is a friend that sticketh closer than a brother."
Proverbs 18:24
Jesus said, "Ye are my friends, if ye do whatsoever I command you."
John 15:14

BIBLICAL FRIENDSHIPS

Learn about friendships in the Bible. Jonathan was a friend of David even though he knew that David would be king instead of him.
Paul and Silas were such good friends that they could even sing together in prison.
Jesus had three special friends in Bethany: Mary, Martha and Lazarus. He raised Lazarus from the dead one day.
Peter's friends prayed for him so diligently that God opened the prison doors and he was released.

GOING CAMPING

FORTY YEARS IN THE WILDERNESS

The longest camping trip on record lasted over forty years. God wanted the Children of Israel to go into the Promised Land. They were afraid because the cities had strong walls and the people were tall. Because they were disobedient, they had to live in their tents in the wilderness for forty years. Usually these tents were made of black goats' skins. Make a tent. Cut one side from a half-pint milk carton. Cover the carton with black construction paper. On the side that has been cut away, slit the construction paper in the center. Fold the paper back for tent flaps.

DO A WILDERNESS FINGERPLAY

Make up verses to tell about the events of the Children of Israel in the wilderness. Use this pattern.

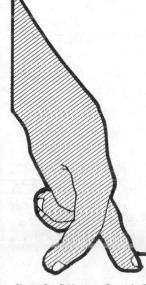

Here we are going out of Egypt.	(Walk the fingers rapidly
Here we are going out of Egypt.	across the table.)
Here we are going out of Egypt	
Into the wilderness.	(Shade eyes and look outward.)
Out in the morning picking up manna.	(Stoop over and pick up
Out in the morning picking up manna.	items and put them in an
Out in the morning picking up manna	imaginary basket.)
For our evening meal.	(Eating motion.)
See us grumble like old grouches.	(Hands on hips—Mean
See us grumble like old grouches.	expression on the face.)
See us grumble like old grouches	
Out in the wilderness.	(Hand above eyes looking outward.)

CAMPFIRES

PETER WARMS HIMSELF BY THE FIRE

After Jesus was arrested, Peter wanted to know what was happening but he didn't want people to know who he was. He stayed a long distance from Jesus and warmed himself by a fire. To try to go un-noticed, he sat with the servants who were discussing and watching the events of the trial of Jesus in the palace of the high priest. Make a campfire and tell this story from Mark 14:53-72.

Glue four twelve-inch sticks together at the top. Wrap red cellophane around the sticks. Add more sticks or twigs to the out-side. Place an electric light inside for more effect.

SLEEPING AROUND YOUR CAMPFIRE

The Israelites did not have nice, cozy sleep-ing bags to use on their trip. At night they just wrapped their outer garments around them to keep warm. Make sleeping bags for your camping trip. Take a piece of quilted fabric 15 inches long and 10 inches wide. Cut off the corners so it makes a nice long oval. Fold the bottom up ¾ of the way. Glue around the edges. Draw a picture of each child. Cut it out and slip it inside the sleep-ing bag.

PILLAR OF FIRE

". . .the Lord went before them by day in a pillar of a cloud, to lead them the way; and by night in a pillar of fire, to give them light; to go by day and night." Exodus 13:21 Because there were no highway signs to guide the Israelites on their camping ven-ture, God used a pillar of fire to guide them at night. This was probably the world's big-gest spotlight. It burned for forty years.

VOICE FROM THE FLAME

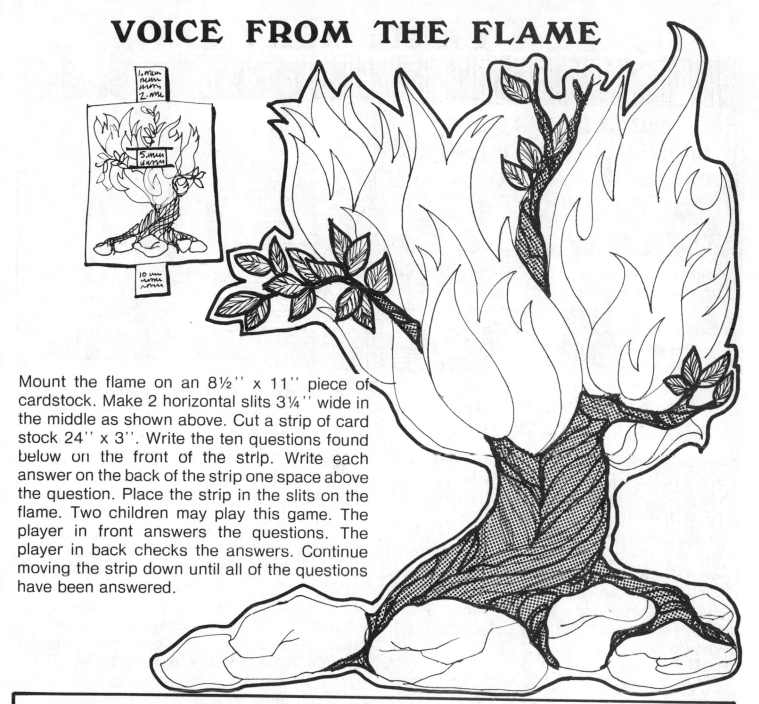

Mount the flame on an 8½'' x 11'' piece of cardstock. Make 2 horizontal slits 3¼'' wide in the middle as shown above. Cut a strip of card stock 24'' x 3''. Write the ten questions found below on the front of the strip. Write each answer on the back of the strip one space above the question. Place the strip in the slits on the flame. Two children may play this game. The player in front answers the questions. The player in back checks the answers. Continue moving the strip down until all of the questions have been answered.

1.	Who appeared to Moses in the fire?	The angel of the Lord
2.	Who spoke to Moses from the fire?	God
3.	What article of clothing was Moses told to remove?	His sandals
4.	Why was Moses told to remove his sandals?	The ground was holy.
5.	What did God tell Moses He saw in Egypt?	The suffering of the people
6.	What did God want to do for the Israelites?	Rescue them from slavery and give them their own land
7.	Who did God want to send to Egypt?	Moses
8.	What was the first sign God gave to Moses?	His staff became a snake.
9.	How was Moses' hand used to show God's power?	It became leprous and God made it well.
10.	Who thought he could not speak well enough?	Moses

GETTING READY FOR SCHOOL

THE CLOTHES THAT DIDN'T WEAR OUT

''. . .I have led you forty years in the wilderness: your clothes are not waxen old upon you, and thy shoe is not waxen old upon thy foot.'' Deuteronomy 29:5

Imagine wearing the same clothes for forty years. If these garments could talk, they would have a very unusual story to tell! Have the children select a piece of clothing that the Israelites may have worn. Personify this article and tell a story from its viewpoint.

JOSEPH'S GENEROUS GIFT

''To all of them he gave each man changes of raiment; but to Benjamin he gave three hundred pieces of silver, and five changes of raiment.'' Genesis 45:22

Joseph's wealth in Egypt was evident because he gave each of his brothers a change of raiment. But to Benjamin he gave five changes of clothing. Benjamin must have been overjoyed at this unexpected gift. Have the children pantomime the story in Genesis 45 placing special emphasis on Benjamin's reaction to all of his new clothing.

ANCIENT CLOTHING

Clothing for the people of long ago was very simple. They had few garments. The inner garment was like our undershirt. It could be made of leather, linen or wool. It could have sleeves, or it could be sleeveless. Some people had inner garments that reached only to their knees. Rich people had garments that reached to their ankles. This was the only garment poor people owned. However, most people owned at least one outer garment. This would be like a bathrobe to us. Many people used this garment as a blanket at night. Have the children wear bathrobes for a day for all activities. At the end of the day, discuss the problems they encountered with this kind of clothing.

GETTING CLOTHES READY FOR SCHOOL

Shopping for clothes for school can be exciting when we realize how many colors, styles, and textures we have from which to choose. As the children look at one another, have them identify all the differences in the clothing of their friends. Have them count the number of changes of clothing they have in their own wardrobes. Compare this to the average wardrobe of the ancients.

SETTING A POSITIVE TONE FOR THE BEGINNING OF SCHOOL

POSITIVE SELF-CONCEPT

Make a mobile showing positive attributes of each person. Trace a silhouette of each child's head. Have the children add interesting shapes to the mobile to represent their good qualities. For example: Heart—shows love for family, hand—good helper, foot—eager to run errands, light bulb—has good ideas. Hang these mobiles from the ceiling.

Section the bulletin board to allow space for some of the children to place pictures and stories about events or circumstances in which they felt they did an excellent job. Have other children add short positive notes to the board stating things they appreciate about the individuals. Examples: Jan is my best friend. Sandi is kind to animals. Bobbie always has a smile. Change the names after a week or two until each child has had a spot on the board.

REACH FOR A STAR

Words and Music
by
Kathy Jones

SEPTEMBER

SCHOOL

1 Make a list of Biblical jobs.	**2** Find a tax collector in the Bible.	**3** Celebrate Labor Day	**4** Identify Simon's job. Acts 9:43	**5** Discover who sold purple dye. Acts 16:14.	**6** Look for a Biblical musician.
7 Find the first mentioned hunter. Genesis 10:9	**8** See how much laborers were paid. Matthew 20:2	**9** Pray for workers.	**10** Find out what Philip's job was. Acts 21:8	**11** Make a set of trivia questions about jobs.	**12** Assume a new job at home.
13 Do all of your chores well today.	**14** Think about the job you would like to have.	**15** Find out what job your dad likes best.	**16** Thank God for your grandparents.	**17** Invite your grandparents to your house.	**18** Write a letter to your grandparents.
19 Find one Biblical grandmother.	**20** Identify one Biblical grandfather.	**21** Have your parents tell you about Athaliah. II Kings 11:1-20	**22** Draw a picture of your grandparents.	**23** Give your grandparents a hug.	**24** Think about how wonderful God made you.
25 Identify six good things about yourself.	**26** Learn Psalm 139:14a.	**27** Plan how to have a good school year.	**28** Learn how to become a U.S. citizen.	**29** Learn how to become a citizen of heaven.	**30** Thank God for adopting you as His child.

CELEBRATE LABOR DAY

"Thus the heavens and the earth were finished, and all the host of them. And on the seventh day God ended his work which he had made; and he rested on the seventh day from all his work which he had made."

Genesis 2:1-2

THE ORIGINAL LABOR DAY

God created the first Labor Day when He rested on the seventh day. He knew how important it was for man to have rest one day a week. He set the example at the very outset of creation. The people did not always follow this example so He included it in the Ten Commandments. Teach the children the fourth Commandment from Exodus 20:8-11.

LABOR DAY IN THE UNITED STATES

Labor Day is celebrated in the United States on the first Monday in September. It was started because many factory owners required the people to work excessively long hours with very little time off to rest. Originally the day was celebrated with a big parade, picnics and fireworks. Now Labor Day is set aside for the worker to enjoy in his own individual way. Make a list of the different occupations of the children's parents in the class. Ask how they observe Labor Day.

WORKERS IN THE BIBLE

Many kinds of jobs are mentioned in the Bible. See how many different ones can be found. Try to identify one person who had this job.

1. Doctor
2. Tax collector
3. Fisherman
4. Shepherd
5. Cup-bearer
6. Tent-maker
7. Hunter
8. Seamstress
9. Soldier

Answers: 1. Luke, 2. Matthew, 3. Peter, 4. David, 5. Nehemiah, 6. Paul, 7. Nimrod, 8. Dorcas, 9. Joshua.

GOOD WORKER

TO: _____

BECAUSE:

_____
Signature

LEARN ABOUT SOME BIBLICAL TRADES

THE CARPENTER

"The carpenter stretcheth out his rule; he marketh it out with a line; he fitteth it with planes, and he marketh it out with the compass . . . ."
Isaiah 44:13

This Scripture gives us the names of some of the tools the carpenter used in Biblical times. The most famous carpenter in the Bible was Jesus. While the carpenter's tools were not advanced, his skill was precise. There was a great need for plows and yokes for farmers. Parts of houses were also made by the carpenters: doors, roofs, and window frames. Carpenters also made some simple household furniture.

Your young carpenters will enjoy making a wooden holder for hot pans. From scrap lumber cut a 7'' square. Cut two 6'' and two 5'' pieces of wood ½'' wide. Glue these strips to the bottom of the square. When the glue is dry, stain the square.

THE POTTER

". . . I went down to the potter's house, and, behold, he wrought a work on the wheels."
Jeremiah 18:3

Jeremiah, the prophet, tells about visiting a potter in Jerusalem. A family learned the skill and passed it on to the children. The clay was first worked with the feet to make it the right consistency for shaping. The potter then placed the clay on his wheel. As the wheel turned, the potter shaped the clay into the desired form. Using potter's clay, make a coil pot. Roll a piece of clay into a long coil. First, wrap the clay in a circle forming the bottom. Then bring the clay upward to form the sides. With damp fingers smooth the clay, especially in the areas between the coils. Allow to dry. Bake the pot in a kiln.

AN ANGRY METAL WORKER

Men have been working with metal since very early times. In Genesis 4:22, Tubal-Cain is referred to as an instructor of every artificer in brass and iron.

When the Israelites were in their Promised Land, the Philistines limited the number of people in the metal working trade because they did not want the Israelites to make swords or spears. The Israelites had to go to a specific town to have their tools sharpened. One metal worker was enraged by Paul's preaching. The silversmith, Demetrius, earned his living making silver gods and goddesses. Paul told the people that gods cannot be made with hands. Allow the children to act out this dramatic story as you read it from Acts 19:24-41.

TRY HAGGLING WITH A MERCHANT

The market place was an important part of the merchant's business world. The market was not always open nor was it operated at the same place. However, it was in operation when there was an item to be sold. No fixed prices were given to any of the items. Instead a process of haggling was used. The merchant began this process by asking a very high price for his product. The buyer offered a very low price for the product. Then the bargaining process began. The merchant came down in his price and the prospective buyer came up in his price. This process continued until they reached an agreement. To help children understand this process, have them bring small items from home which they are no longer using. Have them use the haggling process to exchange the items.

BIBLICAL WANT-ADS

Make up several descriptions for Biblical jobs to be placed in the "Help Wanted" section of the newspaper. Samples are included below.

Man to build very large boat;
Must like animals.

Man to tell Gentiles about Jesus;
Must be willing to take much abuse and be imprisoned if necessary.

Brave woman to save the Jews from being killed. Must risk life by going to the king uninvited. Apply at the Persian palace.

Seamstress to make clothes for needy people. Must be kind, considerate and patient at all times. Apply in Joppa.

Tax-collector to become a disciple of Jesus. Long hours—no overnight lodging will be provided. Must be willing to endure hardships.

Bold, outspoken preacher to prepare the way for the Messiah. Must be willing to dress simply and eat locusts and wild honey.

Encourage the children to write more ads. When enough are accumulated, a game could be played. Make a trail as shown. The players take turns reading the ads and trying to name the person to whom the ad refers. If a correct answer is given, the player may move one space. The first one to reach the end is the winner.

BACK TO SCHOOL

"Get wisdom, get understanding: forget it not; neither decline from the words of my mouth."

Proverbs 4:5

BIBLICAL SPELLING

Make an alphabet booklet by finding a word in the Bible that begins with each letter of the alphabet. Write a short sentence about the word.

A	angels	Angels sang for the shepherds.
B	barns	The rich man wanted to build new barns.
C	camped	The Israelites camped in tents.
D	day	God rested on the seventh day.
E	eyes	Jesus healed the eyes of a blind man.
F	father	We should love our Father in heaven.

BIBLE READING

MY READING RECORD	
DATE	SCRIPTURE

Using a children's version of the Bible, embark on a plan for the children to read small sections of the Bible daily. The goal should be to read one book through in a specified time. Younger children could be read to by a family member. Make a take-home chart with the daily assignments. The sections should be initialed as they are completed. At the end of the time, the chart should be returned. Each person completing a chart should be given a Good Work Card.

1	2	3	4	5
6	7	8	9	10
11	12	13	14	15
16	17	18	19	20

BIBLICAL MATH

Numbers are often used in the Bible. Make a chart with numbers up to 20. See how many passages in the Bible use each number. Write the passage on a small card and place it on the chart by that number. Older children could be taught how to use a concordance to find the numbers.

10 God gave 10 Commandments.
12 Jacob had 12 sons.
6 God made the world in 6 days.
20 If 20 good people could be found, God would not destroy the city.

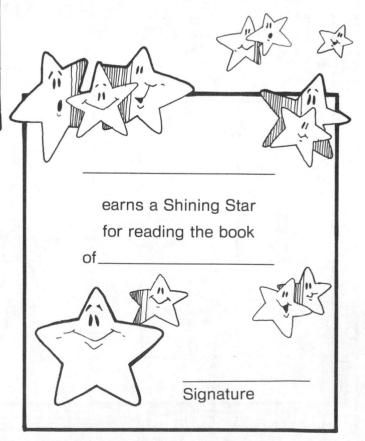

_____

earns a Shining Star

for reading the book

of _____

_____
Signature

BIBLICAL SCIENCE

Write riddles about animals in the Bible. If possible, have a picture of the animals. Have the children match the riddle to the picture. Some animals could include:

1. Animal that talked to Balaam.
2. Insect that John the Baptist ate.
3. Animals David cared for when he was young.
4. Green animals that flooded the land of Egypt during a plague.
5. A coin was found in this animal's mouth.
6. Daniel was thrown into a den with these animals.

SING A SONG

The Psalms were the songs which the Jews used for praising God with singing. Select a familiar Psalm and recite it in a chant.

"The Lord is my shepherd; I shall not want. He maketh me to lie down in green pastures: he leadeth me beside the still waters." Psalm 23:1,2

SOCIAL STUDIES FROM THE BIBLE

Young children study the family and community. List some community workers in your area. List some community workers that are found in the Biblical community. Compare them to see what jobs are similar and which ones are entirely different.

Our Community	Bible Community
Banker	Banker
Grocery clerk	Merchant in market place
Jeweler	Silversmith, Goldsmith
Farmer	Farmer
Tool Salesman	Blacksmith
Tax collector	Tax collector

JESUS IN SCHOOL

When Jesus was a child, He was no doubt sent to a synagogue school. The Bible was the one textbook which the students used. They had to memorize large portions of Scripture. When the student was about 15 years old, he began to study theology from the Talmud. There was probably a great deal of oral recitation in these schools with the teacher saying a line and the pupils repeating it. Use this technique for teaching one lesson to acquaint the children with this style.

Today's Gonna Be a Good Day!

Words by DON MITCHELL

Music by DON MITCHELL and TOM BROOKS

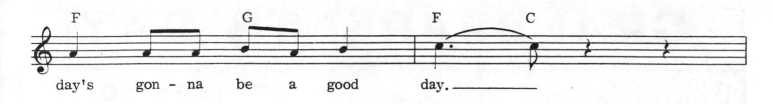

day's gon - na be a good day. _____

ev - 'ry - thing's go - in' my way. I feel

hap - py and high, _____ no clouds in the sky, _____ To-

day's gon - na be a good day! _____ To - day,

is gon - na be _____ a good day!

2. I start to school early I just couldn't be late
   'cause my best friend is waitin' at the school yard gate
   The classroom bully's home with a stomach ache
   Today's gonna be a good day!
   Math class is over I can hardly wait
   it's 11:45, it's my lunch hour break
   I check my lunch box, find some angel food cake
   Today's gonna be a good day!

3. I gotta get movin' I've got places to go
   first my friends and I are going to see a picture show
   Then we're gettin' out our kites 'cuz the wind's gonna blow
   Today's gonna be a good day!
   If you start out the day with a song in your heart
   you'll look foward to the day before it even starts
   If you give the world a smile, and just do your part
   you'll help make each day a good day!

Shining Star Publications, Copyright © 1985, A division of Good Apple, Inc.

GRANDPARENTS' DAY

HONOR GRANDPARENTS

Set aside a special day in September to invite the children's grandparents to school. Make room for them to sit near their grandchildren. Encourage them to assist the children with the day's assignments. Provide a time for each child to introduce his grandparents to the class. Having lunch in the school cafeteria will be a treat for the grandparents and their grandchild. Near the end of the day, have the grandparents tell how their schools were different from the one they experienced today in terms of assignments, appearance of the room or discipline. They might each share one of their school experiences. A short program involving all of the children could culminate the day.

LETTERS TO GRANDMA

Start a grandparent-grandchild pen pal correspondence. Even if the grandparents live in the same city, they will enjoy reading about what is happening in their grandchild's life. Send a cover letter with the first correspondence to explain your goals so the grandparents will be sure to answer the letters promptly.

WHO IS MY GRANDMOTHER?

Make up clues concerning Biblical grandmothers. Give only one clue at a time until the children guess who the grandmother is. Some samples include:

SARAH
My grandmother thought she would never have a child of her own.
She was over ninety years of age when my father was born.
My father's name is Isaac.
My name is Jacob.

RUTH
My grandmother used to live in the land of Moab.
She went to Israel with her mother-in-law, Naomi.
My son's name is David.
My name is Jesse.

RACHEL
My grandmother was loved so much by my grandfather that he worked 14 years for her.
She thought she would have no children.

She was overjoyed when my father was born. His name is Joseph. She also gave birth to my uncle, Benjamin.
My name is Ephraim.

CELEBRATE CITIZENSHIP DAY

TWO HOLIDAYS BECOME ONE

At one time Constitution Day was celebrated in the United States in the month of September. This was a day in which Americans reflected on the freedoms guaranteed by our constitution. Another holiday called "I Am an American Day" was celebrated in the month of May. This holiday was to honor those who had just become citizens of the United States. In 1952, these two days were merged into one holiday. Now many aliens become citizens on this day.

MEET NATALIA

NATALIA BECOMES A CITIZEN

When Natalia was born in a South American country on October 27, 1979, she was loved very much by her mother. However, because the family was very poor, they realized they could not give her the opportunities they would like to provide for her. The parents learned of an adoption agency that would find a good home for Natalia. Back in the United States there was a couple who wanted a child to love. They had applied to the agency a few months beforehand. Many papers had to be filed to assure the South American country that a baby would be well cared for and loved. The couple had to provide information to both the United States government and also the South American government that they could provide for the financial, social and spiritual needs of a baby. One day they received a long-distance telephone call announcing that a little girl was available for adoption. Natalia's new parents flew to South America to get her. Although Natalia entered the United States in 1979, she did not become a citizen until September 11, 1984. On this day her new parents stood with her in court and promised to teach her the rights, responsibilities and privileges of being a citizen of the United States. With this action Natalia's South American citizenship was dissolved, and she became a citizen of the United States.

I'M THE ONLY ONE LIKE ME

Words by Don Mitchell
Music by Don Mitchell and Tom Brooks

I'm the on-ly one like me, I'm the on-ly one like me. An-oth-er me you'll nev-er see, I'm the on-ly one like me.

1. Red hair on my head and freck-les on my face, my best friend Bob, beats me when we race, I can't read as well as my girl friend Grace, but I'm the on-ly one like me. Teach-er can't you see there's a com-pli-ca-ted me sit-ting in that chair un-der all that hair. I hope you re-a-lize that in this small dis-quise may come the hope for peace in our so-ci-e-ty.

2. I'm not as tall as Sue, I'm not as smart as Kim, I have a scar on my nose, and a dim-ple on my chin, some peo-ple say I'm la-zy but they like my sil-ly grin, I'm the on-ly one like me. So when you're down and out and feel-in' kind of blue, when you think it does-n't mat-ter what you feel or do. Re-mem-ber what I've taught you as I sing this song to you. you're the on-ly one like you

You're the on-ly one like you, you're the on-ly one like you. An-oth-er you just would-n't do, You're the on-ly one like you. You're the on-ly one like you, you're the on-ly one like you.

OCTOBER

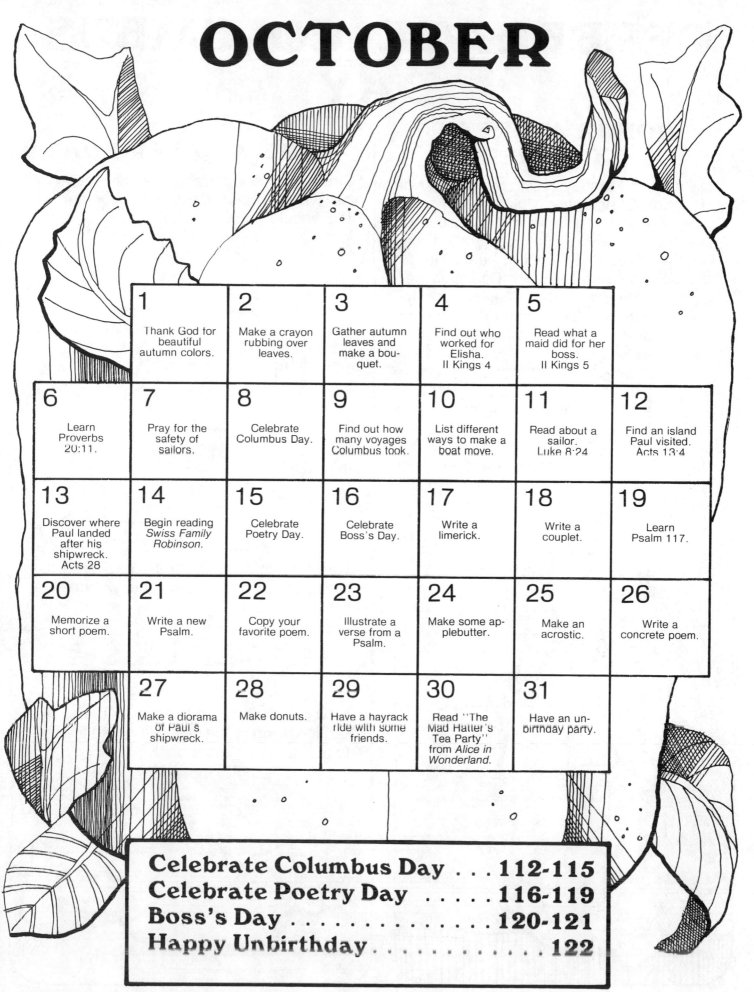

1	2	3	4	5
Thank God for beautiful autumn colors.	Make a crayon rubbing over leaves.	Gather autumn leaves and make a bouquet.	Find out who worked for Elisha. II Kings 4	Read what a maid did for her boss. II Kings 5

6	7	8	9	10	11	12
Learn Proverbs 20:11.	Pray for the safety of sailors.	Celebrate Columbus Day.	Find out how many voyages Columbus took.	List different ways to make a boat move.	Read about a sailor. Luke 8:24	Find an island Paul visited. Acts 13:4
13	14	15	16	17	18	19
Discover where Paul landed after his shipwreck. Acts 28	Begin reading *Swiss Family Robinson*.	Celebrate Poetry Day.	Celebrate Boss's Day.	Write a limerick.	Write a couplet.	Learn Psalm 117.
20	21	22	23	24	25	26
Memorize a short poem.	Write a new Psalm.	Copy your favorite poem.	Illustrate a verse from a Psalm.	Make some applebutter.	Make an acrostic.	Write a concrete poem.
27	28	29	30	31		
Make a diorama of Paul's shipwreck.	Make donuts.	Have a hayrack ride with some friends.	Read "The Mad Hatter's Tea Party" from *Alice in Wonderland*.	Have an unbirthday party.		

CELEBRATE COLUMBUS DAY

HONOR A GREAT EXPLORER

The second Monday in October is set aside to honor Christopher Columbus, who is given credit for discovering our country. The first Columbus Day celebration was held in 1792. One hundred years later, it was again celebrated when Benjamin Harrison was President. It has been celebrated annually since 1921. Although our country is not named after Columbus, there is a country in South America that honors him with the name Columbia. In the United States, many cities, rivers, and streets bear his name. This is the only patriotic holiday which our South American friends join with us in celebrating. Use a large map of the United States or an atlas to find as many cities as possible which are named for Columbus.

MAKE A PAPER BOAT

First fold a double sheet of newspaper in half with the open edges on the bottom. The fold should be on the top.

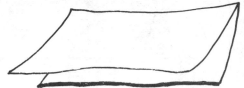

Next fold points A and B diagonally down to point C.

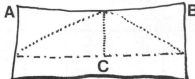

Fold the bottom part up over the front and the back.

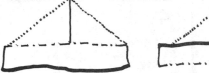

Turn the front points to the back and the back points to the front. This will make a hat.

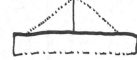

Next pull the two ends and slip the center section down in the middle. Crease the bottom. You now have a boat.

PAUL
FOUND A NEW LIFE

WAS PERSECUTING
CHRISTIANS

COLUMBUS
FOUND A NEW LAND

WAS SEARCHING
FOR RICHES

COLUMBUS FINDS A NEW LAND

When Columbus landed in the New World, he thought he was in the Indies near China. He was confused about his position. People later learned that he had discovered a new land. We are told that we have a new land in heaven. Draw a map showing the way to heaven. Remember there is only one way. Jesus said, ". . .I am the way, the truth and the life: no man cometh unto the Father, but by me." John 14:6

SAUL FINDS A NEW LIFE

When Saul was persecuting and killing Christians, he was also confused. He was a Pharisee who hated the followers of Jesus. He had been successful in driving the Christians out of Jerusalem. Now he wanted to follow those who had left the city and were preaching about Jesus. His plan was to capture them and return them to Jerusalem in chains. His plan was thwarted when a bright light shone on him as he was approaching the city of Damascus. Jesus spoke from the light. Saul recognized Him as the Messiah and his Savior. Because Saul had been blinded by the light, his friends had to lead him into the city. There he prayed and asked God to forgive him. His life was transformed, and his name was changed from Saul to Paul.

Write a recipe for Saul's old life. Write another recipe to include the ingredients God put into his new life.

ANCIENT SEA TRAVEL

Sea travel in ancient times was very risky. Sailors had no charts or compasses to help them. Ships were easily blown off course. Mariners seldom ventured out to sea during the winter months. To maintain maximum safety, ships often traveled as close as possible to land. Sometimes the passengers came ashore to spend the night because the ships were so small. In the New Testament, the islands of Crete and Cyprus were great shipping centers. Although the ships had sails, many of them were propelled by oars.

SAILING, SAILING

Paul was an adventurous sailor like Columbus. On his first missionary tour, he sailed across the Mediterranean Sea to Seleucia and then back to the island of Cyprus. Enlarge a map of the area using an opaque projector. Cover the map with clear adhesive plastic. Give each child a small paper boat. As you tell the stories of Paul's missionary journeys, allow the children to sail their boats in that area.

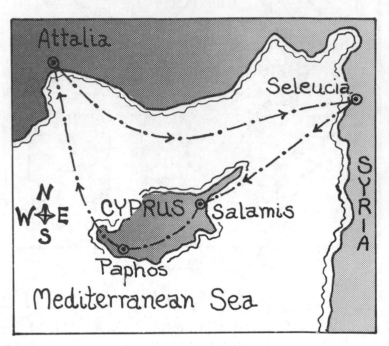

PAUL VISITS MANY CITIES

Remarkable miracles took place in many of the cities where Paul visited. Assign each child a different city to learn about, and have him/her draw a small picture to place on the enlarged map to illustrate an event in this city. Parental assistance should be requested for this project.

EXCITEMENT ON PAUL'S FIRST MISSIONARY JOURNEY

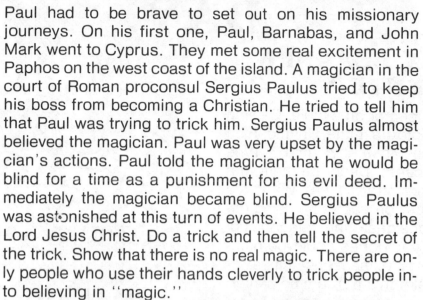

Paul had to be brave to set out on his missionary journeys. On his first one, Paul, Barnabas, and John Mark went to Cyprus. They met some real excitement in Paphos on the west coast of the island. A magician in the court of Roman proconsul Sergius Paulus tried to keep his boss from becoming a Christian. He tried to tell him that Paul was trying to trick him. Sergius Paulus almost believed the magician. Paul was very upset by the magician's actions. Paul told the magician that he would be blind for a time as a punishment for his evil deed. Immediately the magician became blind. Sergius Paulus was astonished at this turn of events. He believed in the Lord Jesus Christ. Do a trick and then tell the secret of the trick. Show that there is no real magic. There are only people who use their hands cleverly to trick people into believing in "magic."

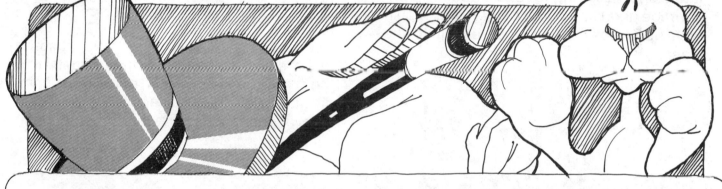

PAUL THE GREAT SPEAKER

Make a colorful face mask of Paul on poster board. Attach a wooden dowel to the back of it so it can be held in front of the speaker's face. Paul never allowed an opportunity to speak for Christ to pass him by. He spoke to rulers Felix, Festus, and Agrippa. He also talked to women's groups, people in jail, and the common people. After you have told these stories on different occasions, have the children retell parts they remember using the mask of Paul as they speak.

SHIPWRECKED

On the way to Rome, the ship on which Paul was a prisoner ran into a storm. The crew lightened the ship for safety, but the storm raged on for many days. All hope was gone that they would survive. However, Paul had prayed, and God had answered his prayer. Paul told the men that the ship would be lost, but not one man's life would be taken. A few days later, all 276 men made it safely to shore. No one escapes frightening episodes in life. Prepare a plan of assistance for times when the children encounter frightening experiences. Follow Paul's example of praying.

Shining Star Publications, Copyright © 1985, A division of Good Apple, Inc.

CELEBRATE POETRY DAY

MAKE A LEARNING CENTER

Arrange a poetry center on a table. Caption it "Come and Enjoy a Little Rhyme. You May Read These Most Any Time." Type poems on 5 x 8 cards. Decorate them with drawings or appropriate stickers. With a felt pen, draw a border on each one using different colors to designate the categories of the poems. The categories could be patriotic, animals, people, seasons, cities, or special days. Make this a free time center. It does not take long to read a poem. To encourage good use of the center, you should pick up a poem often and read it to the class.

MAKING POETRY COME ALIVE

Use seasonal poems. Have the children make small scenes on a table illustrating their favorite ones. This could be an individual project, or several children could be grouped together to work on one poem.

PATTERN POETRY

After the children have read many of the poems in the poetry center, encourage them to select one to use as a pattern. They should change the animal, city, or circumstances. However, many of the same words could be used. Add these pattern poems to the center for the other children to enjoy.

PSALM 150

This Psalm is a very happy one which gives praise to the Lord. Read it several times discussing how God is being praised. Have the children write Psalm 150 personalizing it and showing how they can praise God.

PSALM 136

Choral reading is a natural way to read this Psalm. Assign the first part of each of the odd-numbered verses to one group. Assign the first part of each of the even-numbered verses to another group. Have everyone chorus the last part of each verse: "For his mercy endureth forever." The first nine verses would be appropriate for very young children.

I AM A POET

By writing my thoughts in an unusual way
I produced a really great poem today.

_____
Name

_____
Date

_____
Signature

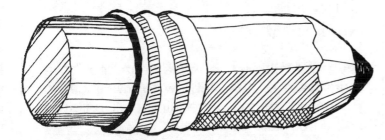

LEARNING POETRY

Select a poem you want the children to learn. One that has a good rhythmic pattern is more fun. Read it several times. Start leaving out words. The children should be able to supply the missing words. Leave out larger portions each time until the poem is memorized. Come back to it often at odd moments so the children will not forget it.

Other approaches:

Have the children pantomime the poem as it is read.

Assign a line to each child who may say the line when you read it. Section it off for a choral reading. Chant it with the children.

WRITING CONCRETE POETRY

A concrete poem is one that is written in the shape of its subject. By drawing an outline of an easily recognized shape and then writing the poetry around this shape, more success will be attained by beginners.

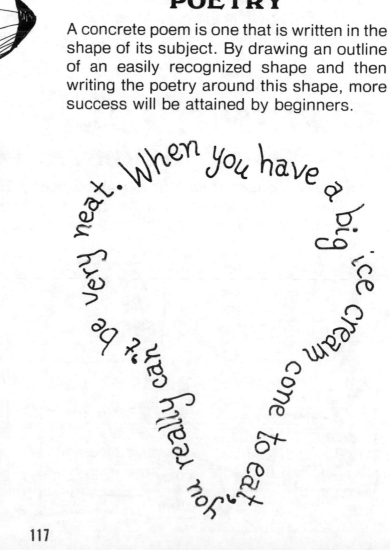

FINISH THE RHYME

Give children the first line of a couplet. They should think of a line to complete it. Some samples include:

Samson was a very strong man

_____

Ruth was as kind as she could be

_____

When Jesus was a little lad

_____

Paul was let down over the city wall

_____

MY FAVORITE POEMS

Provide a book with empty pages. Encourage the children to copy their favorite poems into it. These may be shared with their friends by putting them out to read during silent reading time.

HEBREW POETRY

Hebrew poetry seldom rhymed. Poets used a technique called parallelism. In this type of poetry, the idea was stated. It was then restated in a different way. Sometimes the second statement meant the same as the first. Often an opposite statement was given. The Psalms and Proverbs provide many examples of this kind of poetry.

Stated in the same way:
''A froward man soweth strife:
and a whisperer separateth chief friends.''
Proverbs 16:28

Stated in the opposite way:
''A merry heart maketh a cheerful countenance:
but by sorrow of the heart the spirit is broken.''
Proverbs 15:13

Give the children a statement and have them write in this Hebrew form. Since no rhythm or rhyme is required, all children should be able to succeed.

ACROSTIC POETRY

An acrostic was another form of Hebrew poetry. Psalm 119 is an example of this kind of poetry. Each of the stanzas begins with a letter from the Hebrew alphabet. Write acrostic poetry by starting the first word in each line with the letter in the word to be spelled.

David Was a Poet

Words and Music
by
Kathy Jones

BOSS'S DAY

NEHEMIAH'S KIND BOSS

Characters:	Narrator	Nehemiah	Hanani (Hǎ nā´nǐ)	King

Setting: In the king's palace

Scene 1

Narrator: Many years ago God's people, the Jews, had been captured and carried away into foreign lands. A few years later, their new king allowed some of them to return to their homeland. The people who remained in the land were anxious to hear about their friends in Jerusalem. Nehemiah, who was the king's cup-bearer, was especially anxious to hear about the progress in his homeland. One day he had a visitor.

Nehemiah: (Going toward Hanani and hugging him) Hanani, how good it is to see you! How are the people getting along in Jerusalem? Have they rebuilt the city walls yet?

Hanani: I'm sorry to tell you this news, Nehemiah.

Nehemiah: Go on. I must hear it—whatever it is.

Hanani: It is not going well. The Temple has been rebuilt. Services are being held there.

Nehemiah: That's good news! I'm glad my people are worshiping God again.

Hanani: But the city walls are so broken down. It's hard for me to even look at them. They are so crumpled.

Nehemiah: Is anyone working on them to repair the damage?

Hanani: No, the people think the job would be too big. No one wants to have that much responsibility. They feel it is a hopeless task.

Nehemiah: How do the gates look? Have they been fixed yet?

Hanani: Not at all. The gates were burned when our enemies captured us. They still are charred. No one wants to fix them either. I'm sorry to tell you so much bad news, Nehemiah.

Nehemiah: It's not your fault, Hanani. But it does make me feel very sad. (Hanani and Nehemiah both leave.)

Scene 2

Setting: In the palace. Nehemiah is serving the king from a silver tray.

Narrator: Nehemiah went about his job as the king's cup-bearer as best he could. He was usually happy and smiling, but each day it grew harder for him to look happy on the outside when he was feeling so sad on the inside. One day the king noticed his sorrow.

King: Nehemiah, you are always so cheerful, but you seem very sad today. Are you sick?

Nehemiah: No, my lord, I am not sick.

King: Then why do you look so sad? Why are you unhappy?

Nehemiah: (In fear) I am so sorry. I have tried not to be sad when I was serving you, my lord. I know you want your servants to be happy. But some news about my people in Jerusalem has made me feel very sad.

King: What news could be so upsetting to you? Tell me about it.

Nehemiah: The city where my people live is all broken down. Once the walls were strong and powerful. The gates of the city were big and beautiful. They offered protection for my people. Now the walls are broken and the gates have been burned. No one has the strength and courage to rebuild them.

King: Can I help you with this problem? Do you have a request to make of me?

Nehemiah: If it pleases the king, would you send me to Jerusalem so that I may rebuild the walls?

King: How long would this journey take? When would you return?

Nehemiah: I would not be gone long. Many good workers would help me with the job. I know I will be able to return soon.

King: (Thinks about it for a little bit) Nehemiah, you have served me well. You may go on this journey. I will give you soldiers and horsemen to help you on the way.

Nehemiah: And if it pleases the king, could I also ask permission to get wood from the keeper of the forest so I will have timbers to make beams for the gates and walls?

King: Yes, Nehemiah. I will have my scribe prepare a letter so you may take all the timber you need.

Nehemiah: Thank you, my king. You have been very kind. I will return as soon as possible after my mission is completed. May God bless you.

Narrator: Nehemiah's boss had been very kind to him. Nehemiah went to Jerusalem and rebuilt the walls in record time. It took just 52 days.

HAPPY UNBIRTHDAY

COME DRESSED FOR THE PARTY

Each child should come to the party dressed as a Biblical person with one item that would identify that person.

Nehemiah—a cup
Eve—an apple
Joseph—a handful of grain
Pharaoh's daughter—a basket
Peter—a boat or a picture of a fish
Matthew—coins and a tax form

LET'S GET ACQUAINTED

To make a good mixer for the children, write familiar Scripture verses on paper. Cut the verses apart word by word. Post the complete verses in an obvious place on the board or a chart. Give each child several words. The children must look at their words to see what verse they could make. The children then go from child to child exchanging their words for needed words. Only one word at a time may be obtained from any one individual. A return at a later time may be necessary to obtain another word. A prize should be given for the first person to obtain the correct words.

GIFT EXCHANGE

Have each child bring a gift for an exchange. It could be related to a Biblical person if desired. Place numbers on the table. As each child brings his gift, place it on a number on the table. Give the child a different number. Do not put his gift on the same number you gave to him. This will insure that no one will get his own gift. At exchange time call a number and the child with that number may claim the gift placed on the corresponding number on the table.

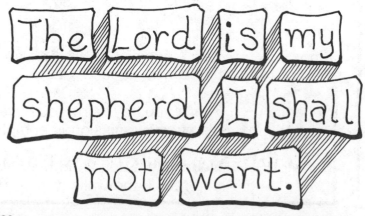

The Lord is my shepherd I shall not want.

NOVEMBER

1	2	3	4	5	6	7
Share your favorite book.	Resolve to read every day.	Ask your parent to read to you.	Tell your favorite Bible story.	Pantomime a story for your family.	Identify your favorite Bible book.	Tell a friend what you are reading.
8	**9**	**10**	**11**	**12**	**13**	**14**
Find out your friend's favorite story.	Find a good book at the library.	Pray for veterans.	Celebrate Veterans Day.	Read about Jacob. II Samuel	Read about Abner. II Samuel	Learn about God's armor. Ephesians 6
15	**16**	**17**	**18**	**19**		
Read about Goliath's armor. I Samuel 17	Find what David did with armor. I Samuel 17	Discover how soldiers helped Paul. Acts 21	Thank God for the beautiful earth.	Enjoy the colors of autumn.		
20	**21**	**22**	**23**	**24**		
Look for colors in the sunset.	Thank God for the wonderful people in your life.	Celebrate Thanksgiving.	See how many different colors you can find.	Start learning Psalm 100.		
25	**26**	**27**				
Thank God you are free to go to church.	Count the freedoms you enjoy.	Thank God for His love for you.				
28	**29**	**30**				
Read Nehemiah 12:46.	Read Psalm 50:14.	How will you be enriched? II Cor. 9:11				

Shining Star Publications. Copyright © 1985. A division of Good Apple, Inc.

CELEBRATE VETERANS DAY

HONOR VETERANS

Veterans Day, on November 11, honors men and women who have served their country in the armed forces. Some people celebrate the day with parades and speeches. A memorial service is held at the Tomb of the Unknown Soldier in Arlington Cemetery. This memorial was first established to honor those soldiers who could not be identified after World War I. The marble headstone of the Unknown Soldier bears this inscription: "Here rests in honored glory an American soldier known but to God."

BE A SOLDIER FOR GOD

"Wherefore take unto you the whole armour of God, that ye may be able to withstand in the evil day, and having done all, to stand."

Ephesians 6:13

To be an effective soldier for God, every part of His armor must be used. This armor is not made of metal or anything material. Rather it is love, salvation, truth, righteousness, faith, peace and the Word of God.

Draw each piece of protective armor that a military soldier must have. Beside it, have the children place the armor a soldier for God must use.

Righteousness   Spirit-Word of God   Salvation

GOD PROVIDES SOLDIERS TO PROTECT PAUL

When Paul was arrested in Jerusalem, because some men did not believe his teachings about Jesus, a great crowd assembled and started a riot. They wanted to kill Paul. However, some Roman soldiers arrived and rescued Paul. The soldiers were going to take him to Caesarea to testify before Governor Felix. In the meantime 40 men had vowed not to eat until they had killed Paul. They planned to ambush him on his trip. Paul's nephew heard about this plot and was able to deliver that message to Paul. God provided 200 soldiers, 70 horsemen, and 200 spearmen to insure Paul would have a safe trip to Caesarea.

Tell this exciting story from Acts 21:1-23:35. Have each child write a story pretending he is Paul's nephew. How does he feel when he learns about the plot against Paul? What problems does he encounter in getting the message to Paul? What are his feelings about the situation?

PLAY THE GENERALS' MARCH

For this game two boundaries are established in the gymnasium or on the playground. The children are lined up behind the starting line. Two children are designated as generals. They stand on the finish line facing away from the other children. The general on the left gives the command to march. All of the other children start to march quietly toward the finish line. The other general may give the command to halt at any time. When this command is given, both generals turn around quickly. Any child they see moving is sent back to the starting line. The generals turn around again, and the command to march is given. The first two children to cross the finish line become generals for the next game.

MAKE ENLISTMENT POSTERS

Give each child a 12'' x 18'' piece of construction paper. Have him make a poster to advertise enlistment in God's army.

GOD NEEDS YOU!

JESUS HEALS A SOLDIER'S SERVANT

When Jesus came to Capernaum, a centurion asked Jesus to heal his servant who was very sick with palsy. Jesus told the man He would go to his house and heal the servant. The centurion recognized the tremendous power of Jesus and said that He could heal him without going to the house. Jesus gave the centurion a wonderful compliment for this statement. Tell this story from Matthew 8:5-13. Have the children pantomime the story as it is told.

THANKSGIVING

GOD SENDS SQUANTO TO HELP THE PILGRIMS

In 1621 the Pilgrims had a bountiful harvest because their friend, Squanto, had taught them how to grow foods in the new land. He had also taught them how to catch fish and trap animals. When the days of harvest were completed, Governor Bradford announced that they would have a day of thanksgiving. The Pilgrims invited the nearby Indians. Chief Massasoit and ninety of his people came for the feast. They stayed for three days. They enjoyed some sports and contests and a lot of good food. Because there were so many Indians, Chief Massasoit sent his braves into the woods to capture game for the feast. The Indians and Pilgrims were even closer after this special feast. Governor Bradford said that Squanto ''was a special instrument sent of God for their good.''

Sometimes we forget to thank God for the wonderful people He sends to help us. List the people who help us in some way. Thank God for all of these people.

THE FEAST OF THE TABERNACLES

''. . . in the fifteenth day of the seventh month, when ye have gathered in the fruit of the land, ye shall keep a feast unto the Lord seven days: on the first day shall be a sabbath, and on the eighth day shall be a sabbath.'' (Leviticus 23:39) Among the first celebrated Thanksgivings was the Jewish Feast of Tabernacles. On the first day, they were to take boughs of trees and palm branches and make little booths to live in for seven days. This was to remind the people that God had brought them out of Egypt. The feast lasted for eight days—from one Sabbath to the next. It was a time of rest and fellowship. This feast must have been fun for the children. Make little booths using shoe boxes. Cover the outside with small branches. Cut out figures of children to place inside the boxes.

GOD'S COLORFUL BRUSH PAINTED THESE

BLUE

RED

GREEN

PINK

PURPLE

ORANGE

YELLOW

THANK GOD FOR BEAUTIFUL COLORS

Think of a black and white world. How dull this would be! God wanted us to have beauty all around us so He created colors. Give children magazines to find colors in God's creation. Cut out the items and place them on the proper section on the bulletin board. Remember to thank God for providing us with so many beautiful colors.

THANK GOD FOR VARIETY IN FOODS

How would you like to have oatmeal for breakfast, lunch and dinner every day? It would not be a very exciting menu to anticipate. God wanted us to have choices and beauty in our foods. Start making a list of the different foods that children have eaten. When a child has a food that is not already on the list, add it on that day. Make another list of foods the children haven't eaten but are available for them to eat. Thank God that He has given us so many choices of good things to eat.

THANK GOD FOR THE BEAUTIFUL EARTH

''They go up by the mountains; they go down by the valleys unto the place which thou hast founded for them.''   Psalm 104:8

How uninteresting our world would be with no hills or valleys. Make a collection of pictures of land formations that make our world beautiful. While including favorite vacation spots of the children and interesting places they have visited, do not forget to remember the beauties around home that can be enjoyed every day. Thank God for these places of beauty that He has created for us.

LEARN THE THANKSGIVING PSALM, PSALM 100

MAKE A JOYFUL NOISE UNTO THE LORD

Music and Words by Kathy Jones

Make a joy-ful noise un-to the Lord

Make a joy-ful noise un-to the Lord

Sing a song from your heart; Come a-long Do your part.

Make a joy-ful noise un-to the Lord

Rainbows Dreams and Butterfly Wings. Copyright © 1983. Good Apple, Inc. Box 299. Carthage, IL 62321-0299

''Make a Joyful Noise unto the Lord'' will help the children learn the first verse of Psalm 100. Assign different children or groups of children to draw pictures illustrating the rest of the verses. Place the pictures in the proper sequence on the wall to provide a visual clue in learning the Psalm.

THANK GOD FOR SEASONS

"He appointed the moon for seasons: the sun knoweth his going down." Psalm 104:19
Thank God for the seasons. He provided a time of work and a time of rest for all of His creation. Read about God's wonderful planning in Ecclesiastes 3:1-8,11.

A TIME FOR EVERYTHING

Divide the class into four groups. Have the groups recite the passage from Ecclesiastes in the following way.

All:	To everything there is a season, and a time to every purpose under the heaven:
Group One:	A time to be born,
Group Two:	and a time to die:
Group Three:	a time to plant,
Group Four:	and a time to pluck up that which is planted;
Group One:	A time to kill,
Group Two:	and a time to heal;
Group Three:	a time to break down,
Group Four:	and a time to build up;
Group One:	A time to weep,
Group Two:	and a time to laugh;
Group Three:	a time to mourn,
Group Four:	and a time to dance;
Group One:	A time to cast away stones,
Group Two:	and a time to gather stones together;
Group Three:	a time to embrace,
Group Four:	and a time to refrain from embracing;
Group One:	A time to get,
Group Two:	and a time to lose;
Group Three:	a time to keep,
Group Four:	and a time to cast away;
Group One:	A time to rend,
Group Two:	and a time to sew;
Group Three:	a time to keep silence,
Group Four:	and a time to speak;
Group One:	A time to love,
Group Two:	and a time to hate;
Group Three:	a time of war,
Group Four:	and a time of peace.
All:	He hath made everything beautiful in his time.

GOD PROVIDES FOR TWO WOMEN

Naomi and Ruth were two poor women who came to Bethlehem about the time of the barley harvest. Ruth went to the fields of Boaz to glean. God provided for them bountifully. Tell the story from the book of Ruth. Make one large face of Ruth and one of Naomi. (P. 131) Place these on a bulletin board. Make 20 sheaves of grain. Write a statement on each sheaf. Provide an answer key. One child should read the information on the sheaves. If the information is true of Ruth, place the sheaf under her face. If it is true of Naomi, place the sheaf under her face.

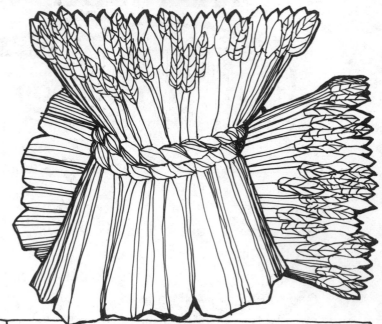

NAOMI

1. She left her homeland because of a famine.
2. She was the wife of Elimelech.
3. She was the mother-in-law of Ruth.
4. Her husband and two sons died.
5. She decided to go back to her homeland.
6. She took her daughter-in-law to Bethlehem.
7. She had a rich kinsman.
8. She said, ''Boaz is my kinsman.''
9. She told Ruth to go see Boaz one evening.
10. She became the nurse for Boaz's child.

RUTH

1. Her homeland was Moab.
2. She was loyal to her mother-in-law.
3. She arrived in Bethlehem with her mother-in-law at barley harvest time.
4. She wanted to leave her homeland to follow God.
5. She said, ''Let me go into the field and glean.''
6. She went to the field of Boaz.
7. She gleaned about a bushel of barley one day.
8. She gleaned with the maidens of Boaz.
9. She married Boaz.
10. She had a son named Obed.

GOD HELPS ME

Have the children think of times when they needed something and prayed to ask God to help them. Have them record how God provided help for them. Post these on the wall for all to read.

GOD PROVIDES

God helped me by _____

_____

I know He loves me.

_____
Signature

NAOMI

RUTH

CELEBRATE CHILDREN'S BOOK WEEK

MEET MY BOOK FRIENDS

Henry Huggins

John D.
Mary W.
Susie B.

Esther

Mary W.

Laura

Diane W.
John D.
Susie B

Shan

Mary W.
Susie B.

Enlarge pictures of characters from children's secular books or Bible story books. Place these on the classroom walls or in the hall if space is limited. Write the name of each person under his/her picture. Place a caption over the pictures: How Many of My Friends Do You Know? Under each person place a signature sheet. If a child knows this person either from having heard the story or from reading it himself, he may write his name on the signature sheet. Encourage the children to read about the unfamiliar characters.

READ OUR PATTERN STORIES

Develop a pattern story for all of the children to enjoy. Tell the story of Daniel and how he bravely honored God even when he and his friends were thrown into a fiery furnace. Be very specific on details. Have each child write a story using this pattern but changing the main character and the circumstances. Each child could use himself as the main character. Before the child starts to write, help him decide on the following:

Time the story took place.
Action for the story.
Law character disobeyed. Action taken against him/her by the ruler. How character was rescued.

Bind the completed stories into a booklet for everyone to read.

ENCOURAGE HOME READING FOR THE FAMILY

Send home a list of stories for parents to read the children. Have each child bring from home an item that was in the story the parents read on the previous night. Some examples:

For the story of Samson—a jar of honey.

Paul being rescued by being let down over the city wall—a small basket.

When Jesus fed the multitude with loaves and fishes—a loaf of bread.

Allow the children to guess which story was read. Play a game patterned after Twenty Questions. In this game children ask questions that can be answered with a yes or no. If the correct answer has not been obtained after twenty questions, the child should reveal the correct story.

DATE	MINUTES READ
1.	
2.	
3.	
10.	

BEDTIME STORIES

To encourage reading before going to sleep, make a reading chart for the children to record the nights they read at least ten minutes. After ten days have the children return the chart to school. Award them with a 100 Minute Good Work card or reading ribbon award.

I TAKE A GOOD BOOK ALONG

_____

has read at least one hundred minutes

from _____ until _____

_____
Signature

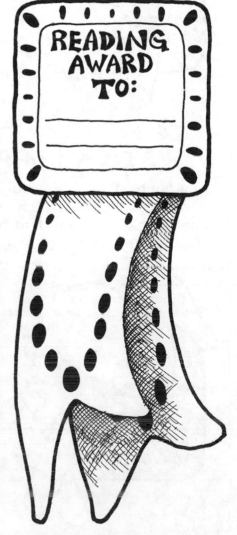

READING AWARD TO:

_____
_____

SHARE STORIES WITH PUPPETS

FINGER PUPPETS

Make finger puppets to help children retell their favorite stories. These could be drawn by the children, or pictures could be cut from used Sunday School material. Tape the figures to the children's fingers. Instruct them to move their fingers as they tell their stories. This will create action.

SOCK PUPPETS

To make a sock puppet, cut a slit in the toe portion for the upper and lower parts of the mouth. Sew red felt in this section for a tongue. Add facial features with felt pieces. Almost any animal can be made this way.

STICK PUPPETS

Any figure may be cut out and glued to a dowel or ruler. The puppeteer may move this puppet any way that is desired. This style is very simple for young children.

BASIC FORM PUPPET

Cut two basic shapes from felt. The size will depend on the span of the child's hand. The small finger and thumb slip into the arms of the puppet. The other three fingers will hold the head. Make sure the puppet is small enough for little hands to reach this far. Glue around the edges of the basic shapes leaving the bottom portion free. Allow the glue to dry. Add facial features with felt and yarn to create a person or an animal.

DECEMBER

		1 Thank God for His promise.		
2 Celebrate Advent.	3 Learn about Fanny Crosby.	4 Find out about your missionaries.		
5 Start learning Luke 2.	6 Write some braille letters.	7 Learn about Corrie ten Boom.		

8 Show love to someone.	9 Pray for missionaries.	10 Make a Christmas card in braille.	11 Learn about A. Wetherell Johnson.	12 Read about the Quakers.
13 Make an African village.	14 How many hymns can you find by John Wesley?	15 Give a gift to a needy person.	16 Learn a new Christmas song.	17 Make a poster of the birth of Jesus.

18 Learn about David Livingstone.	19 Compose a Christmas poem.	20 Make a gift for someone special.	21 Thank God for winter.	22 Write an invitation for Jesus to come to your house.	23 Thank God for sending Jesus.	24 Pray for ones who do not know Jesus.
25 Celebrate Christmas.	26 Enjoy God's love by sharing it.	27 Tell about your favorite gift.	28 Remember to write thank-you notes.	29 Thank God for this year.	30 Plan a New Year's party.	31 Attend a Watch Night Service.

Shining Star Publications, Copyright © 1985, A division of Good Apple, Inc.

CELEBRATE ADVENT

Advent is a religious observance which includes the four Sundays before Christmas. The word is derived from a Latin word that means "a coming." Advent reminds us of the coming of Jesus. The first Advent is the birth of Jesus. The Second Advent will be the coming of Jesus as King and Judge. Advent should be a happy season in which people anticipate the birth of Jesus.

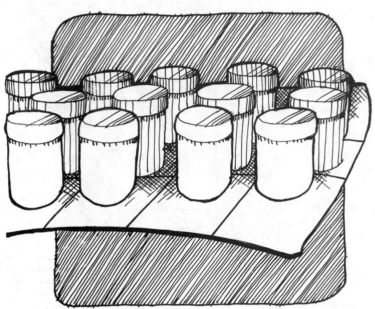

ASSEMBLE AN ADVENT TABLEAU

Establish an area where a tableau may be placed. Discuss with the children the items that are needed. Have children volunteer to bring the items as they are suggested. One child may bring straw, another could bring small boards for the stable, another one could bring a clay animal or person. Build the tableau adding just one item a day. Each child should be encouraged to contribute something. On the last day, add the baby to the manger.

ADVENT CALENDAR

Make a table calendar using poster board and small plastic bottles with white lids. Draw the squares for the days on the calendar. Glue the bottom of each bottle onto a day on the calendar. Write the number of the day on the lid of each bottle. Place a Scripture verse into the container. Verses from Luke 2 would be ideal. Include a treat in each bottle. At the beginning of each day, allow a different child to open a container. The older children may read the verse. You should read it for the younger children. If possible, encourage the children to learn the verse for the day. Each day review the previous verses. The child who opened the container should be allowed to have the treat for that day.

CELEBRATE FAMOUS CHRISTIANS

CORRIE TEN BOOM

The story of Corrie ten Boom as told in *The Hiding Place* has liberal amounts of excitement and intrigue. This story would best be told using parts that are appropriate for young children. As the story unfolds, have the children make a mural depicting the different phases of this remarkable woman's life. Because her house was so unusual, the children might enjoy making a simple model of it. This could be accomplished by using three shoe boxes.

A. WETHERELL JOHNSON

A. Wetherell Johnson was the founder of the largest Bible study organization in the world, Bible Study Fellowship. When she was young, she was an agnostic. After she became a Christian, she went as a missionary to China. When she could no longer serve as a missionary, she came to America. Her Bible study was started unintentionally. However, her small start was so successful that more and more people wanted to be involved. Her story is told in the book *Created for Commitment* by A. Wetherell Johnson. Start the children on a planned Bible study to help establish a lifetime pattern.

THE BLIND POET

Fanny Crosby is the author of thousands of hymns even though she was blind since she was six weeks old. Her first piece of poetry was written when she was only eight years old. Fanny had such a pleasant disposition and a great love for God that her blindness seldom seemed to be a handicap. Rather, she used it as a stepping stone to her next adventure for God. She was active until she was ninety years old. Sometimes she used braille to help her learn. Teach the children some of the braille symbols. Then write Bible verses in braille.

Braille alphabet :

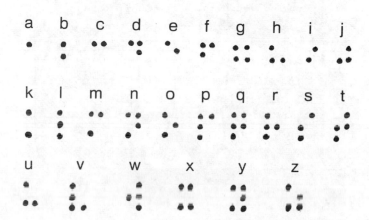

WILLIAM PENN

William Penn was a Quaker who founded Pennsylvania. He always believed in an individual's right to worship as one pleased. He became a Quaker when he was 22 years old. Because this church was not the state religion in England, Quakers were scorned, imprisoned and sometimes put to death. William Penn was in prison three times for writing and teaching about Quakerism. The English King, Charles II, owed Penn's father a large sum of money. William Penn asked for land in America to pay the debt. The king gave him land which is now called Pennsylvania. People from all over Europe came to the colony for religious freedom. Quakers were known for their simple lifestyles and plain clothing. One little Quaker girl wanted to have bright and fancy clothes. However, an event changed her mind and helped her to realize that her Quaker dress was the best one after all. Read *Thee Hannah* by Marguerite DeAngeli.

DAVID LIVINGSTONE

David Livingstone gave 33 years of his life in helping Africans physically and spiritually. He also had a great curiosity and explored many regions in Africa. He spoke against slave trading and was able to reduce the practice. As a doctor, he treated many severely ill Africans. His gentle manner and respect for all people endeared him to those for whom he worked. He was known for setting goals and taking steps to attain those goals. He had a great faith in God and lived his faith on a daily basis. His life had many exciting episodes. Tell his story. Make a little African village the way it might have looked when Dr. Livingstone was there. Use milk cartons to make little grass huts. Use clay to make the people and animals.

JOHN WESLEY

John Wesley was the founder of the Methodist church. His mother thought religious education was very important. She started to teach him the alphabet as soon as he could walk. He started to read the Bible at a very young age. When he was 5 years old, his house burned down. He was the last person to be rescued. He considered this to be a miracle from God. He established many churches and went on horseback to visit them as often as possible.

CELEBRATE CHRISTMAS
MAKE A SPECIAL GIFT

Make a Christmas booklet for each child by decorating two pieces of 10'' x 14'' construction paper. Laminate these pieces or cover them with clear plastic adhesive. Attach the two covers with colorful library book tape on the outside. Place masking tape to reinforce the covers on the inside. Fold five sheets of 18'' x 12'' paper and sew them inside the booklet. Use the first page as the title page. On consecutive days tell the following stories or read them from a children's Bible story book. Have the children write their versions of the story on lined paper. When the stories have been proofread and corrected, glue each one to one page. Opposite this page have each child draw a picture to illustrate the story. When all stories have been completed, wrap the booklets for the children to give to their parents for Christmas gifts.

Story 1 Angel Gabriel Visits Mary

Story 2 Angel Gabriel Visits Joseph

Story 3 The Trip to Bethlehem

Story 4 The Birth of Jesus

Story 5 The Shepherds Visit Jesus

Story 6 Jesus Is Dedicated in the Temple

Story 7 The Wise Men Worship Jesus

Story 8 The Flight into Egypt

Story 9 How My Family Celebrates Christmas

A few samples of the children's work are given to help you with this project. These were written by third grade children. For younger children the story could be written on the board for them to copy.

Story 1

A VISIT FROM HEAVEN
By Stephanie H. age 8

Ever since Adam and Eve sinned, the world had been looking for a Messiah. At just the exact moment, Gabriel appeared. The angel knew the right place, the right house, and the right bedroom. When Gabriel flew into her house, Mary was very surprised.

"You are favored," he said. "You are going to have a son."

"I cannot have a son. I am only engaged to Joseph," she said.

"The Holy Spirit will come over you and your child will be the Son of God. Are you willing to do this?"

"Oh, yes. I would be honored." Gabriel left very quickly. Mary was left wondering, but happy.

Story 4
THE CHRIST CHILD

by Sean E. age 8

When Joseph and Mary arrived in Bethlehem, they were exhausted. They looked for an inn. The innkeeper said he was sorry but the rooms were full. Then he noticed that Mary was going to have a baby. He offered them a stable. Mary's heart sank—an old smelly stable! There was no other place except it. Joseph went in with his lantern. He said, ''There's some fresh straw over here.'' Then the baby arrived. A few animals were there. Cows mooed. Horses neighed. They were the only ones to welcome Him. If I had been there, I would have praised Him.

Story 5
The Shepherds Welcome Jesus

by Michael T. age 8

One starry night the shepherds were out in the fields tending their sheep when suddenly an angel appeared. The shepherds were very scared, but the angel told them not to be afraid.

''I have good news for you to spread around. The Savior has been born in the stable behind the inn,'' said the angel. The shepherds stared in amazement. Then the sky was full with angels singing, ''Glory to God in the Highest. Peace on Earth and goodwill to men.'' Then, as fast as they had come, all of the angels were gone! The shepherds ran as fast as they could to the smelly stable and explained everything to Joseph and Mary. The shepherds fell to their knees worshiping Baby Jesus. The next day the shepherds ran all over telling people about the good news. Some ran to the stable to see Jesus, but still others just went about their work not caring about the news. Those that didn't care were missing out on something very, very big!

Story 8
The Narrow Escape

by Shane B. age 8

King Herod waited for the wise men to return. But they never came. An angel told them not to go back to Herod because he would kill the baby. At first Herod wasn't worried about it. King Herod sent some messengers to Bethlehem to find the wise men. When the messengers got to Bethlehem, they found the wise men had left without telling anyone. Oh, how furious Herod was! He called the soldiers, and he said to kill all the babies under the age of two. An angel warned Joseph about this terrible thing. The angel said to go to Egypt. Mary and Joseph packed their bags and left as quickly as possible. It was a narrow escape, but God protected Jesus.

WE WORSHIP HIM, TOO

Cover the bulletin board with blue butcher paper. Enlarge the figures of the Biblical characters and place them on the board. Have the children draw pictures of themselves. Add these to the bulletin board.

START TRADITIONS

Start Christmas traditions and observe them each year in your classroom or school. Some suggestions include:

Make a decoration for the home that is symbolic of the real Christmas.

Recite parts of Luke 2.

Illustrate Luke 2.

Have a birthday party for Jesus.

Make an ornament for the tree that tells of the birth of Jesus.

WE THREE KINGS

Tell the story of the wise men visiting Jesus from Matthew 2:1-11. Use the pantomime from *Acting for God* by Kathy Jones. This is a Shining Star Publication.

Shining Star Publications, Copyright © 1985, A division of Good Apple, Inc.

REWARD GOOD BEHAVIOR

Cut a strip of felt 36'' long x 5'' wide. Use a large needle to sew thirty 10-inch pieces of yarn at regular intervals down the felt. Tie a candy cane on each section with the yarn. Observe good behavior in the class. At the end of the day, allow one or two children to take a candy cane from the felt strip.

A
CHRISTMAS GIFT
FROM
YOUR TEACHER

TURN THIS BELL
IN FOR ONE
FREE HOMEWORK
ASSIGNMENT

_____
NAME

IS A SHINING
EXAMPLE OF A
GOOD CITIZEN

Date

Signature

ROLE PLAY THE CHRISTMAS STORY

Go through the Christmas story with the children role playing the characters. The second time have the children change the story by deciding what they would do if they had been the characters in the Bible story.

CHRISTMAS FUN

Pin the name of a person or object on the back of each child. The child must then go to the other children and ask questions about his tag. When he has enough clues, he may make a guess about his object or person.

CHRISTMAS CARD BOOKLETS

Collect old Christmas cards. Make small booklets from the pictures for young children. Encourage them to tell the story shown on each picture.

CHRISTMAS CARD ART

Carefully cut the figures of identifiable objects from Christmas cards. You now have two stencils. Hold one of these securely on a sheet of paper. With a sponge which has been dipped into poster paint, stroke the paint on the outside edges of the stencil. When finished, lift the stencil off the paper. After the paint is dry, write a Christmas greeting on the back of the card.

MAKE LEARNING SCENES

Cut out the figures from old Christmas cards. Stiffen them by gluing a Popsicle stick to the back of each figure. Make a base for each one from a Popsicle stick. Arrange the figures to make a scene. Have the children find a Scripture which tells about the scene. Write the verses on sentence strips to lay in front of each group of figures.

LISTENING CENTERS

Enlarge pictures from Christmas cards. Use these to identify the listening centers. Tape record appropriate stories for each of the centers. Set up listening centers for the children. If headphones and recorders are available, several stations may be used at one time.

WITHIN A LOWLY STABLE

Words and Music by Kathy Jones

Verse 3. Within a lowly stable was heard a distant bell.
Within a lowly stable the story shepherds tell.
Kings would bow before Him now; He would be called E-man-u-el.
Within a lowly stable was heard a distant bell.